PERCY BEALE NEAME AND THE SHEPHERD NEAME BREWERY FAVERSHAM

1836 - 1913

JOHN OWEN

MMXIV

Typeset in Berkeley LT 10pt by Mickle Print (Canterbury) Ltd, Canterbury, Kent
Printed and bound in Great Britain by Mickle Print (Canterbury) Ltd, Canterbury, Kent

A catalogue record for this title is available from the British Library
ISBN: 978-0-9559997-8-9

Foreword

Jonathan Beale Neame

Percy Beale Neame is a figure who looms large in the collective memory of the Neame family, even though no one alive today ever met him.

This excellent book uncovers many new facts and lays to rest many myths that have built up over the years.

As one of his great great grandchildren, and as Chief Executive of Shepherd Neame today, I am fascinated by this study of his life, his personality and his business career.

The essence of the business that he built up remains today : an integrated brewery and pub business, a strong freehold pub estate, a passionate commitment to beer quality, a strong and active involvement with Faversham and Kent community. His love of sport in general and cricket in particular, is alive and well, as the company today is principal sponsor of Kent County Cricket Club and many local village sides.

Percy was clearly a shrewd financier and very sound buyer of pubs. He clearly understood the value of a strong cash flow, for to transform the business with high indebtedness to a much stronger freehold business with more manageable levels of debt, over his lifetime, was a considerable achievement. Many of those pubs remain key assets in the business today.

I also find it fascinating how many of the challenges he faced then are similar to those of today: the challenges of sourcing product and quality raw materials, the sensitivity of the market place to economic peaks and troughs, the constant change in consumer lifestyles and drinking habits. Some of his letters to suppliers or customers or tenants could easily have been written within the last few years!

At his death in 1913, he was a highly respected local figure who had built up a small fortune and a great business with a strong reputation. The local community, the company's employees and members of the Neame family continue to benefit from his legacy today.

In many respects however, the great burden of sustaining this fell to his son Harry, who had the unenviable task of keeping the family and business together during the First World War and its painful aftermath, when both consumption of beer fell and taxes increased sharply, and in spite of losing both his brothers within a few months of each other in 1916.

I am very grateful to John Owen for his diligence and perseverance in research, his enthusiasm for all things related to Shepherd Neame, and of course for his outstanding scholarship. Without him, so much of our collective history would be lost.

Acknowledgements

Firstly, I must thank Jonathan Neame for his unfailing encouragement to me in researching this history and then getting this book published. On many occasions I have probably disturbed his train of concentration on a current business problem with my questions or discoveries. So often the past seemed, however, to be mirrored in his current deliberations.

Bobby Neame, his father, has been a constant source of recollection and anecdote about both the family and the business.

Other members of the Neame family have contributed also. The late Mary Dawes was most forthcoming about her grandmother, Madame. George Barnes copy of 'The Barnes Saga' was illuminating with his late father's view on his Neame uncles and aunts. Sandys Dawes, Mary Tapp and Barbara Tapp have loaned family photographs for inclusion.

For the use of many of the original sources I have to thank The Kent History and Library Centre at Maidstone; the Cathedral Archives at Canterbury; the University of Kent, Canterbury, newspapers collections; Corpus Christie College, Oxford, Library ;the Probate Court in the Strand; and The National Archives, Kew.

The most important original source is of course the archive which is still with Shepherd Neame Ltd at The Brewery site. To this I have had unlimited access.

My especial thanks go to Mrs Pru Stokes of Biddenden, who alerted me to the collection of Beale Family letters, which she has calendared and allowed me to use.

Those others who have helped I hope I have thanked in the relevant footnotes.

Dr Richard Baker and his colleagues at Achievements, Northgate, Canterbury, have printed out my research into the immediate members of the family of Percy Neame in the pedigree attached.

My sincere thanks go to Kayley Middlebrook and Tim Ashenden of Mickle Print, Canterbury, for the time spent in ensuring this production looks as professional and fresh as it does.

Finally, I would like to remember two other friends; the late Dr Theo Barker who 16 years ago opened the door into the rich history of England's oldest brewery; and the late Alan Neame, that great preserver of Neamiana, who would have added pithily to, and no doubt chuckled at, this work.

CONTENTS

Introduction

Percy Beale Neame is most remembered as the man who gave his surname to a brewery whose brands flourish worldwide today. To his descendants he is remembered as the name sitting at the top of the family tree, which hangs in the board room, and from whom the shares many of them still enjoy descended. In his home town of Faversham in East Kent he is immortalised in the portrait photograph of a benign looking late Victorian countryman wearing a shooting jacket.

Little impression of Percy Neame survives, for here is a man who joined a provincial brewery 150 years ago in 1864, who died 100 years ago in 1913 and whose last surviving granddaughter died in 2012. It is surprising that there are no myths or legends about someone who lived to be 77 and who ran a business for 49 years; other than that he was always referred to in the family as the Master and his wife as Madame.

Percy Neame appears to be the classic Victorian entrepreneur. He was the youngest son of a younger son of a younger son with no expectations. At the age of 28 he bought his way into a one third share in The Brewery of Shepherd, Mares and Neame and 13 years later bought out the executors of the remaining partner to become a sole proprietor. When he died he was worth £240,000 and was the richest man in Faversham.

His personality appears to be that of the countryman son of a farmer. He married his second cousin, bought a fine house on the edge of Faversham and had 10 surviving children. He leased two farms which he clearly enjoyed running actively. He was a keen cricketer and much enjoyed fox hunting. He was politically conservative but remained well clear of involvement in party politics or local government.

This is the bare outline of his life but the 'whys' and the 'hows' of his business life are intriguing. Why did he leave farming at a time of prosperity to take on a huge debt in a sector he knew little about? How did he run his business and was he an innovator? In summary why was he a success?

At the death of Percy Neame in 1913 the challenges to the family and the business were greater than during his lifetime. Ownership and the conversion of the business into a limited company had to be agreed by all his children, to whom he had bequeathed equal shares in his estate. Investment in the plant was needed and then came the Great War with all the challenges that brought about for savings, quality, manpower and taxation. Then two of his three sons, who were in the business, died.

Part of the life of Percy Neame can be reconstructed from the business archive at The Brewery. Balance Books, Private Ledgers, General Out-Letter Books and general files have survived in profusion for his life time. What are missing from the collections are all the Private Letter Books, private correspondence and diaries of Percy Neame and his wife. For the private life external local sources, especially local newspapers, have to fill the gap.

What emerges also from these sources is the survival of only one of the five large nineteenth century independent Faversham family businesses, of brick making, cement manufacture, banking, gunpowder manufacture and brewing. By 1910 brick making, cement making and the local bank had sold out and only the later continued in Faversham, as part of a national group. By 1920 gunpowder manufacture had removed to Scotland and in 1927 the competing brewery sold out and ultimately closed in 1990.

The legacy of Percy Beale Neame is the independent Shepherd Neame Brewery still in Faversham on its original site that is now the oldest operating brewery in England and one of the oldest breweries in the world.

CHAPTER ONE

The Neame and Beale Families

The ancestry of Percy Beale Neame was purely Kentish. His paternal Neame ancestors all came from East Kent and his maternal Beale ancestors all came from the Weald of Kent. The Neame ancestors were exclusively farmers but the Beale ancestors were farmers with other commercial interests.

The Neame family emerges at Woodnesborough, near Deal, in Kent, in the late fifteenth century and remained there for five generations. Their home was Ringleton Manor. In the late sixteenth century the senior line died out and a new line was established by a younger son at Rattling Court in the adjoining village of Goodnestone. The senior lines remained there for three generations and then died out in the late sixteenth century. A younger son established another line in the next village of Ickham, at Garrington Court,[1] where the family remained until all descendants of that branch left there by the early nineteenth century. [Neame Pedigree 1][2]

Increasingly large families, with more children surviving into adulthood, could not support younger sons in one village. Better opportunities would always have arisen away from the home base. Changing patterns of agriculture also encouraged migration. Marriages and inheritance of better properties encouraged people to move on. The division of land to all male children equally, according to the Kent law of Gavelkind, would have divided farms theoretically into smaller and uneconomic units but in practice the law usually led to one brother buying out his siblings. As the Neame family were not land owners, but tenants and leaseholders, this would have had little significance for them. Rural populations were mobile.

Until the early nineteenth century the Neames were described as yeoman. This elastic term connoted significant farmers, usually long term tenant farmers of quality land. They were not then landowning or gentleman farmers. It is also interesting that the main line was not armigerous, they did not bear arms. The name does not appear in any of the Kent Visitations of Arms nor are arms displayed on any Neame tombs.

Refer to Neame Pedigree 1 for the family tree of the ancestors of Thomas Neame senior.

Thomas Neame, the grandfather of Percy Beale Neame, was not only a younger son but one who moved some distance away from the old family territory. He moved to Selling, near Faversham, where he founded a new branch of the family which survives locally today. He was about 28. Thomas came to Selling Court, which was part of the estate of Lord Sondes, about 1775. Here was a good quality farm that only a man of some repute would have been allowed to tenant.

He started modestly. In 1777 Thomas rented Selling Court for £55 and 2/3 of the Selling Tithes for £130. By comparison William Hilton was renting Abbey Farm Faversham for £290 and John Bunce was renting Homestall Farm Faversham for £190.[3] By 1779 he was also renting Luton Farm in Selling for about £37 per year.[4] Robert Hilton of Marshes, probably the most prosperous farmer in Selling at that date, was assessed on rents of £251.[5] By 1785 the church had re-valued the tithes as Thomas was paying £200 for the 2/3 part.[6] In 1799 he insured a hop oast, which suggests he was also a hop grower.[7] By 1808 Thomas was in partnership with his second son John. Not only had rents risen but the family holdings had increased considerably. In Selling they were paying annual rents of £110 for Selling Court Farm, £220 for part of Selling and Rhodeborough tithes; and in Sheldwich they were tenanting farms rented at £302 per year and the tithes for £110 per year. By 1811 Little Harefield Farm, Selling, was added to the portfolio at a rent of £150 per year.[8] Working on the assumption of one third of income for rent, one third for re stocking and one third for profit,[9] these figures suggest a gross turnover of about £2,600 per year.

Thomas enjoyed 40 years of prosperity. By 1806 he retired from Selling Court and built a new house, Luton House,[10] on Sondes land. Agricultural returns were excellent. The Great French War produced increased demands and hence high prices for farmers; between the 1780s and early 1800s the prices of wheat and barley doubled.[11]

At the same time Thomas became an agriculturalist and promoter of good husbandry. He was a member of The Kent Society for the Encouragement of Agriculture and Industry and became a member of the committee by at least 1805.[12] In 1802 he was a steward at the Anniversary Dinner, chaired by Lord Sondes, held at the Fountain Inn, Canterbury.[13] His co-steward was John Bax of Preston House, Faversham.[14] By 1807 both Thomas and his younger brother, Austen Neame, were on the committee.[15] Austen was a hop grower, for in 1800 he was noted as a committee member at the General Meeting of the Landowners and Hop Planters of East Kent, together with amongst others John Hilton of Lords, Sheldwich.[16]

Over a lifetime of endeavour Thomas became part of the East Kent establishment by filling the usual parish offices of churchwarden, overseer of the poor and highways surveyor. He also became a member of the Faversham Farmers Club,[17] that convivial forum for informal exchange of ideas on many subjects. Neither he nor his relations filled the county offices of Justice of the Peace or Deputy Lieutenant of the county.

At his death in 1817 Thomas left approximately £15,000 to his eight children.[18] His brother, John, who had continued to farm at Garrington Court until he retired to Canterbury in 1804,[19] left about £11,000.[20] The youngest brother, Austen, and his wife died intestate which suggests they died with little money. His estate was in line with those of other successful local farmers. The subtleties of his success were shown in descriptions of him. In his will he describes himself as gentleman and in his insurance policies he is described as yeoman.

Just as Thomas established the Neame family in Selling, so his children built on that success. Within a generation the Neame family became the major tenant farmers of the Lees Court Estate of the Sondes family. Thomas had one daughter, who married a New Romney farmer, five sons who became farmers and one son who became a Canterbury industrialist. These were the uncles and father of Percy Neame.

Refer to Neame Pedigree 1 for the family tree of the seven children of Thomas Neame senior.

Thomas, the eldest son of Thomas senior, returned to the traditional Neame territory at Chislet to farm. Here he 'played a prominent part in reclaiming the Wantsum Channel and associated marshes...and reclaiming many acres for agriculture from the sea..'[21] He was active in promoting the New Canterbury Corn Market in 1824 by contributing £10[22] and in 1827 he was chairman of the East Kent and Canterbury Agricultural Association.[23] In 1834 he was awarded a prize for his 'long wolled sheep'[24] by the Kent Agricultural Association. In December 1836 he was President of the Kent and Canterbury Cattle Show Dinner.[25] At Chislet he was churchwarden for 7 years and overseer of the poor for 6.[26] Despite a leading profile in local agriculture this was against a background of post war depression and falling agricultural returns. Perhaps that, and the long term nature of returns on draining marshes, explains why he was not as financially successful as his brothers; in 1840 he died intestate.[27]

John, the second son, became at first a partner with his father and then took over the tenancies of all his farms. He continued to live at Selling Court. In 1826 he took over the tenancy of Marshes, newly acquired by the Sondes Estate from the children of Thomas Gibbs Hilton, at a rent of £300 per year. By 1827 he held Sheldwich and Selling Tithes for £350 and farms, including by then

Beacon Hill Farm in Molash, for £809. He was the largest single tenant of the Sondes family and accounted for 11% of their total Kent rental.[28]

At the death of Robert Edmonds in 1825 John Neame became Lord Sondes steward or agent. No greater confidence in his ability and reliability could be shown by one of the largest, reasonably progressive and liberal landowners in the county. The salary of £300 per year was modest but with it came the opportunity to acquire the best farm tenancies and other miscellaneous commercial opportunities. The survey and purchasing of new farms, which forged ahead under the bachelor baron, selecting and granting of tenancies, ensuring agreements were kept, collecting rents, ensuring the welfare of tenants, managing the woodlands, collecting the manorial rents, representing the agricultural interests of land owners in all public forums, keeping abreast of agricultural innovation and supporting the political lives of his employer and his family, were his core duties. Protecting farms and organising security during the agricultural unrest of the 1830s was especially demanding and dangerous. As steward of the Lord of the Manor of Faversham and much creekside property there, he was directly involved with the improvement of the Faversham Creek and the commercial opportunities that would bring to agriculture in the neighbouring farms. His job was no sinecure.

He had to maintain a leading profile in East Kent agricultural circles, for upon the profits of agriculture the wealth of his employer depended. In 1822 he joined with his brothers and many others in East Kent to lobby Sir Edward Knatchbull about agricultural distress in the county.[29] In 1825 he attended meetings to promote a Faversham stock (cattle) market. In 1827 he was chairing meetings of the East Kent and Canterbury Agricultural Association.[30] From 1834 he was active, as the agent of Lord Sondes, at meetings concerning the Commutation of the Tithes.[31] In 1838 he appeared before the Commission on Church Leases.[32] From 1844 he was representing himself and Lord Sondes at meetings discussing the building of railways.[33] From the 1830s he was active in the promotion of the improvement of the Faversham Creek by cutting and dredging. In 1847 he was part of a local deputation to the Chancellor of the Exchequer.[34] He catered for moral welfare, always a branch of good estate management, by membership of the Committee of the District Society for the Promotion of Christian Knowledge in 1826.[35]

His other business interests were equally local. From 1816-1842 he was the agent of Corpus Christie College, Oxford, for their farms in Selling, Sheldwich and Chilham.[36] In 1828 he became a director of the newly formed Upper Scray Division Friendly Society, under the patronage of Lord Sondes.[37] He was a shareholder in the Kent Fire Office, with two of his brothers[38] and by 1836 he was a director.[39] In Selling he filled the traditional parish roles of churchwarden, from 1828 to 1845, and of overseer of the poor.[40] Both roles were concerned as much with keeping costs down as looking after the church and the poor; further examples of good estate management.

At the same time John Neame was an active farmer. By 1840[41] he was grazing sheep on 93 acres of Hernhill Marsh, 50 acres at Hope and 63 acres at Staple. At Selling he was farming 400 acres of mixed arable and pasture and 64 acres of hops. At Sheldwich he farmed 207 acres, at Leavland and Badlesmere he farmed 73 acres and at Chilham he had a further 22 acres. In all he farmed nearly 1,000 acres. In 1836 he and his brothers were subscribers to the Kent and Canterbury Cattle Show, where he was showing his rams[42] and winning an award for his cattle.

However, he was a conventional conservative protectionist of the landed interests,[43] despite the rural unrest he saw around him. In 1830 his barn and contents were set alight by an incendiary but thanks to the Faversham dredgers and his labourers the fire was put out. This suggests that he was at least a fair employer. A few weeks later he attended a meeting at the Ship Inn at Faversham where the raising of a troop of volunteer cavalry under the command of Lord Sondes' brother was proposed.[44] In 1839 another fire destroyed 3 tons of his hay in Selling Court.[45] In 1845 he signed the Kent petition against the amendments to the Corn Laws and personally sent copies to the newspapers and the West Kent Protection Association.[46]

Beyond his work his interests were also local. From the 1830s he was a subscriber to the Canterbury Races, held each year on Barham Downs.[47] At the March meeting of the Faversham Floral and Horticultural Society in 1839 he won the best prize.

After a relatively long and certainly public life John Neame died at Selling in 1849. His personal estate was sworn at £25,000.[48] It was divided nearly equally between all his children. Albeit that his interests were much wider than those of his father, it is probably no surprise that his estate was not greater considering that agricultural prices had halved since 1817.[49] His eldest son Frederick Neame took over many of his father's farming interests, but moved to Macknade. His third son remained at Selling Court. His second son Harry, also a farmer, who had married Mary Anne Collard of Chislet, had died in the previous year. Their daughter received her late father's inheritance of £2,000. That daughter, Florence Neame, grew up to marry her first cousin once removed, Percy Beale Neame.

Charles, the third son of Thomas Neame, had a career in farming very similar to that of his brothers, albeit less public than that of John Neame. By 1820, and probably before the death of his father, he was the tenant of Great and Little Harefield Farms in Selling. These were both quality farms leased by Lord Sondes from Corpus Christie College and sub let.[50] By 1827 he too ranked as one of the major tenants of the estate.[51] By 1839 he tenanted 350 acres in Selling and Sheldwich from Sondes and a further 179 acres in Goodnestone and Preston from Mrs Simpson of Cooksditch, Faversham.[52] In addition he was a landowner as well as a tenant; the first of his family to become so. By 1839 he owned 200 acres of marshland in Graveney and 2 acres in Selling. By the time of his death he owned 636 acres.[53]

Charles was an active farmer and member of the Faversham Farmers Club[54]. His activities were mixed. He was a grazier, a cattle farmer, hop grower and arable farmer. In 1839 at Harefield he had 41 acres of hops.[55] In Graveney and Goodnestone marshes his pasture supported both cattle and sheep.[56] In 1822 he took a prize for his sheep. From at least 1836 he was an annual subscriber to the Kent and Canterbury Cattle Show.[57] In 1841 his ploughman won a prize and he won a prize as a hop dryer.[58] In 1846 his shepherd won a prize at the Faversham Agricultural Society Dinner.[59] In 1854 at the Smithfield Club Cattle Show he and his son won a silver medal and £10 prize for their pure breeds class 17.[60]

He was as active in agricultural politics as were his brothers. He signed the letter to Sir Edward Knatchbull in 1822 about agricultural distress. He was a conservative protectionist and also signed the East Kent Agricultural Association Petition against the Corn Law in 1845. In 1847 he was one of the deputation to the Chancellor of the Exchequer. In 1851 he attended the dinner of George Young MP for the Protectionists at the London Tavern.[61] In 1862 he was on the committee for the return of Sir Norton Knatchbull MP.[62]

Charles outlived his four farming brothers and lived to enjoy some of the recovery of English agriculture. His later years were amongst the most profitable peace time years. In his will he left £25,000[63] plus 636 acres of land to his six children. His eldest son, another Charles, of Copton Manor,[64] Preston, clearly enjoyed the full benefits of the later Victorian agricultural prosperity. When he died in 1892 he left £42,000, far more than his two farming brothers.

Robert, the youngest and sixth son of Thomas Neame, nearly escapes history.[65] Like four of his eldest brothers he too was a farmer. By 1820 he was farming jointly with John Neame and on his own account in Selling.[66] He died intestate in 1821, aged only 26.[67]

George, the fifth son of Thomas, was the only son to find a career outside farming. His choice and no doubt drive made him the most financially successful of all his family contemporaries. About 1810 he was apprenticed to a Canterbury tallow chandler and soap maker. By 1824 he had taken over the business at 24, St Margaret's Street. He moved to Lambs Lane and then on to the large site fronting the High Street (later the Post Office and now a restaurant) but with the factory behind, fronting Stour Street but running along the banks of the Stour.[68] By 1855 the business was taken over by his eldest son, Alfred.[69]

George, like his elder brother John, was a very public person and deeply involved in Canterbury life and politics. He was mayor of Canterbury in 1836, 1843 and 1851 and alderman in 1843.[70] He was a magistrate for the Home Division and later chairman of the bench and was a Deputy

Lieutenant of Kent for many years.[71] In 1852 he was a member of the committee to return Sir Edward Dering as MP.[72] In 1853 he petitioned against the Canterbury election results, alleging bribery.[73] He was, unlike all his relations, a liberal or Whig.

His politics today would be deemed to sit uncomfortably with his business activities. There were constant complaints about the smell of his soap factory and the contamination of the river. The smell was also driving guests away from the County Hotel (now Abode) opposite. At debates about the depth of the Stour he suggested a river plough be used to clear it. When the City Council was discussing the cholera outbreak in Canterbury he refused to admit there was one.[74]

He was involved actively however in many of the improvements of mid Victorian Kent. In 1824 he contributed to the new Canterbury Corn Market.[75] By 1836 he was a director and shareholder of the Kent Fire Insurance Office.[76] In 1836 he chaired the meeting for the Central Kentish Railway and the Sandwich Harbour Company and insisted that the plans be approved by Sir John Rennie, the engineer of Sheerness Harbour.[77] In 1840 he was a subscriber to the Kent and Canterbury Cattle Show.[78] In 1845 he was a member of the Canterbury Cemetery Company provisional committee.[79] He attended meetings in Canterbury concerning the North Kent Railway Continuation Bill in 1849.[80]

'By steady perseverance he acquired a comfortable independence'.[81] He bought the Tower House, by the West Gate, Canterbury, possibly as early as 1839[82], and restored and extended it for his large family. By 1862 he had retired to the edge of Canterbury, to Prospect House at Harbledown.[83] When he died in 1873 he was the wealthiest by far of all his brothers. His personal estate was valued at £70,000.[84] Of his sons; Alfred, took over the Canterbury business; George Friday Neame ran a very successful timber merchant and brokers company in the City of London and was a deputy chairman of the West India Dock Company; and Albert, a soldier, was court martialled. This branch of the family moved from the land as others were to do later.

Austen Neame was the fourth son of Thomas Neame. He married Anne Beale of Biddenden.

The Beale family, like the Neame family were deeply rooted in Kent, but in West Kent and the Weald. In the late Middle Ages they were Maidstone merchants and port reeves. By the seventeenth century they were clothiers in Biddenden and wharfingers in London. Industry and trade were as important to them as their farming and small landowning interests.[85] They were more an urban family than the country family of the Neames. [Pedigree 3. Beale][86]

Refer to Beale Pedigree 3 for the family tree of the descendents of Richard Beale senior.

By the late seventeenth century they were described as gentlemen and by 1786 Richard Beale senior of Biddenden was described as esquire in his will. That did not disguise the source of his wealth. He lists in a 1784 Deed of Apportionment a quay and a wharf as well as lands in Biddenden, Kenardington and Warehorne on Romney Marsh.[87] By the 1760s Seaman Cooke Beale, his eldest son, was running the wharf, which suggests that at that date this was the main financial interest of the family. He married the daughter of a London merchant, George Speere, of Great Tower Street, at St Leonards Shoreditch. In his will of 1789 he is described not as esquire or gentleman but as wharfinger of St. Saviours, Southwark.[88] His wharf was on the river, in the Pool of London, east of what is now London Bridge Station. The place name survived into the later nineteenth century.[89] His interests were clearly London based and commercial. Richard Beale's younger son, another Richard, probably took over the property in Kent, as he is described as esquire of Biddenden, when he died, childless, in 1814.

Seaman Cooke Beale's eldest son, another Richard, was born in London, but there is no evidence that he followed old family interests in London or at the wharf. The opposite is true. By 1800 he was described as of Omenden in Biddenden and in 1814 he inherited River Hall and the Biddenden lands from his childless uncle Richard. He was typical of the country gentleman who inherited enough money from the commercial endeavours of his forebears, with the land that had bought, to enjoy a pleasant provincial and family life for a generation. He married Frances Witherden, a member of another prosperous Biddenden family.

At his death in 1836 Richard Beale junior is described as Esquire. Richard Beale junior owned River Hall and 186 acres attached, which were in his own occupation. These either included or were in addition to properties called Cot in Cot Lane, Elmstone, Podkin and Wagstaff. In Romney Marsh he owned fresh marsh in Brenzett, Snave and Ivychurch of 218 acres.[90] Other un-named messuages and lands were also bequeathed in his will. His lands possibly totalled 600 acres.[91] He left annuities of £350, a pony and 4 wheeled carriage and £200 to his wife. As a marriage bond of £2,000 to one daughter and £3,000 to another is mentioned, the total value of his estate, if spread equally to each of his children, which is likely, probably totalled about £20,000. His wife Frances died in 1854.

Refer to Beale Pedigree 3 for the family tree of the 10 children of Richard Beale junior.

Richard and Frances had ten surviving children, most of whom were successful but three were distinct failures. These were the maternal uncles and aunts and the mother of Percy Beale Neame.

All but one of the sons became farmers, in and around Biddenden. Richard, the eldest son, inherited the main house and land of River Hall. By 1851 he was a grazier with only one servant.[92] In 1861 he was described as a landed proprietor and farmer of 40 acres.[93] When he died in 1874 his personal estate was listed at a mere £300.[94] He appears to have been estranged from the family.[95]

Seaman, the second son, was the most successful of all the children. In 1841 he was a grazier at Ivy Court in Tenterden.[96] In 1851 he was described as a farmer using 1,200 acres employing 18 labourers and 4 servants. By 1871 he was described as a magistrate and landowner still living at Ivy Court, Tenterden. He married into the Curteis family of Tenterden (who were also related to the Shepherd family of Shepherd Neame Brewery).[97] When he died in 1875 he was described as an esquire and he left a personal estate of £40,000.[98] His son became the first vicar of St Michaels Church, Tenterden.

William, the third son, studied law at The Temple and became a solicitor. By 1841 he was living at 71 King Street, Maidstone. He was still there in 1881, albeit that he was described as a 'Solicitor on the Rolls'.[99] He outlived all his brothers and sisters and when he died in 1889 aged 93 he left a personal estate of £16,000.[100]

Thomas, the fourth son, struggled and then failed as a tenant farmer at a time of widespread agricultural hardship. In 1841 he was at Cocklesden Farm at Goudhurst but in 1851 he was described as 'late farmer' at Marden. In 1861 he was a land agent living in a cottage at Catsfield, Sussex. In 1871 he was the sanitary inspector at Sea Road, Pevensey.[101] He was always in need of financial help from his family and as he died intestate he was probably penniless. His eldest daughter became a home-help and his son an excise officer in Ireland.[102]

Charles, the fifth son, died young about 1837. His widow Mary, who lived for another forty years with her brother-in-law in Biddenden, managed to leave a personal estate of £6,000.[103]

John, the sixth son, was a failure. He was described in 1841 as 'independent' and living with his brother George. By 1861 he was described as a retired farmer. In 1871 he was described as an agricultural labourer with 12 children at Beckley near Chichester.[104] He died soon after.

George Richard Beale was the youngest and seventh son. He never married. He was a farmer by 1841 and lived with his mother at home. By 1861 he was living at Elmstone House, Biddenden as head of the household and was farming 290 acres with 3 men. In 1871 he was described as a grazier.[105] By the time he died in 1880 he had been able to enjoy at least 20 years of profitable farming, which some of his brothers had not. In his will his personal estate was listed at £16,000.[106]

The three daughters of Richard and Frances Beale each married successful husbands; two were Kent farmers and one was a London merchant. Frances, the second daughter, married a local man, Charles Simmonds Pilcher, who was born in Rye. He had varied business interests. In 1851 they lived at Freizingham Farm, Rolvenden. He was described as both a farmer of 500 acres employing 30 men and as a merchant and ship owner employing 21 hands. By 1861 he had retired and he died soon after.[107]

Elizabeth, the third daughter, married John Curteis, another member of that large family from Tenterden. By 1841 they were living at Lawrence Poultney Lane, north of Lower Thames Street, in the City of London, and John was a wholesale grocer. By 1851 they had moved to 2 Gordon Place, near Gower Street in Fitzrovia, where he was described as a merchant. In 1861 he was described as a sugar merchant and in 1871 as a wholesale grocer.[108] John died in 1875, and in his will, where he was still described as a merchant, he left a personal estate of £50,000. His executors were his son in law, John Clarke Crosthwaite McCaul, his brother-in-law, George Richard Beale and his nephew, John Lawrence Graham. Of his generation he was the most successful member of the family, not least because he had left the land for commerce in London.

Anne Beale, the eldest daughter, married the Faversham farmer, Austen Neame.

CHAPTER TWO

Percy Beale Neame Early Years 1836-1864

Austen Neame of Selling married Anne Beale of Biddenden in September 1823 at Biddenden Church. Of their seven children six survived. Austen was dead within fourteen years but his widow remarried and lived for nearly a further forty years, as Mrs Henry Hilton. Of the six children Percy Beale Neame was the youngest, but by far the most commercially successful of them all.

Austen Neame, like his brothers, was born and brought up at Selling Court. There is no record of where he went to school. He probably went to a number of small private schools or, if he were like Henry Shepherd senior, to Ashford Grammar School. He was not at Kings Canterbury and was unlikely to have attended the Faversham Grammar School. He followed his brothers into farming and took over the tenancy of Homestall Farm after the death of the childless Thomas Bunce in 1817.

This was another of the prime and ancient farms of the Sondes Estate. It was on the edge of Faversham, but included some land in Hernhill and Graveney, with fine soil. If the 1839 Tithe Schedule is a guide it had 235 acres of which 208 acres were arable and 26 acres pasture.[109] For a young man of 26 to take over a farm with an annual rental of £450,[110] which was greater than that of any other farm on the estate, reflects how significant the Neame family had become. The patronage of his elder brother, John, as the estate agent, and later that of his son Frederick and grandson Frederick Ivo Neame, together with the reliability of the family to farm well, not only ensured this prize holding but ensured the Neame family retained the best tenant farms in this small area for a century and a half. By 1837 the three Neame brothers accounted for 17% of the total Sondes Kent Rental of £12,000.[111]

Austen, like his brothers, was also deeply involved in the farming world. In 1817 he became a member of the Faversham Farmers Club.[112] In 1822 he and Charles Neame won prizes for their sheep at The East Kent Graziers Show.[113] In 1824 he contributed to the new Canterbury Corn Market.[114] In 1825 he attended the meeting to establish a stock market at Faversham. In 1830 he became a Freeman of Canterbury[115] and was described as a yeoman. He enjoyed shooting.[116] In 1834 with his brothers he was active at meetings concerning the commutation of the tithes.[117] In 1836 he was a Guardian of the Faversham Union Poor House.[118]

Anne Beale was born into the large farming family at Biddenden but one that was a small landowner. Her father was a 'gentleman farmer' but none the less an active farmer.[119] With her brothers and sisters she was sent away to small private schools. In 1813 she was at Prospect House, Tenterden and by 1816 she was at Turret House School in Clapham, for at least two years. Brothers Richard, Seaman and William were all at school in Bromley, Thomas was at Mr Rawes Academy and Charles was at Mr Buckland's in Tenterden.[120] The very few letters of the period relate brother William visiting Anne at school and taking her lip salve in 1817 and in 1820 sending her a parcel of silk and a hat.[121] In 1818 her letters home talk of a problematic neck boil and improvement in the last 2 years.[122] Stray references suggest that a regular and lively correspondence became part of the routine of Anne and most of her family.

There is no indication of how Anne met Austin but by 5 March 1823 she was staying with the Neames. In her letter home she says...'the Neames are very kind with parties...brother Seaman Beale let her down by not coming over but she can look after herself...father will need spectacles... he will not peruse this letter as it will arrive on a hunting morning...' On 11 October 1823 she wrote to her father from Homestall Farm, Faversham, where the marital home was established, '... Miss Neame, Charles, Mary Curteis are staying with Miss Shepherd...very gay with visitors...John Neame people of consequence that keep carriages...bells ringing for them...parties planned... cooking book, games and piano...happy and husband very kind...sending Faversham oysters and walnuts...Mr Neame (her husband Austin) farming...' On 16 October 1823 another letter to her father speaks of ...' the first party date confirmed...parents to stay...will play for them and show the house...please send pheasants and a hare...very happy with Austin...'[123]

Austin farmed at Homestall against a background of agricultural distress and generally poor returns. However, when he died in January 1837, aged 46, he was able to leave a personal estate of about £18,000,[124] in addition to a few farm cottages and 20 acres of land. As he had inherited only £2,000 he had clearly been a successful farmer over 20 years; but he did have the advantage of very fine soil and a tenancy by courtesy of his brother, John Neame, the agent of the landowner, Lord Sondes.

Anne remained at Homestall as a widow. She continued as the tenant and in 1841 she was described as a farmer.[125] Brought up as a farmer's daughter and married to one for 14 years she was clearly capable. She was much helped by the farm bailiff, Edward Swinyard,[126] until 1848[127] when he left. Here all but one of her seven children were born and here the six surviving children were brought up until she remarried, Henry Hilton, in 1844.[128] Thereafter the family moved to his house, Sole Street, Selling, but the farm tenancy was retained.

The use of her maiden name, Beale, as a second christian name for all her children suggests an especially close family.[129] These family attachments may account for her comments in a letter to her mother in 1849.[130] 'Although I am blessed I often have anxieties, for where a woman has six children she must at times feel for them and perhaps they may do wrong, but so far I have been fortunate.'

Refer to Neame Pedigree 2 for the family tree of the 7 children of Austen Neame.

Anne Beale Neame, the eldest child, was born in 1824. She probably had some education at a small private school, as yet unknown.[131] A glimpse into her life is given by the letters she wrote to her grandmother Beale.

Frequent family events and visiting were common. In 1844 she gave a long account of a summer week spent with her father's brother, uncle George Neame, at Canterbury.[132] '...on Tuesday accompanied by mama and sister Fanny we went to the bazaar for the benefit of the Kent and Canterbury Hospital...all articles were worked by different ladies of the neighbourhood and the stalls were kept by ladies...two bands were in attendance...mama left at seven and we dressed at eight thirty... at ten (pm) we made our appearance in the ballroom...nine from our house...a great many of the ? were there...on Wednesday we went to the bazaar again and in the evening we had friends...the bazaar receipts were £1,195 which will repay all the hospital debts...there was a service in the Cathedral and £95 was raised...on Thursday we went to the races...mama came to Canterbury as uncle George offered to drive her in her chaise to the races...I went in uncles carriage...other cousins on horseback...we dined at 7...on Friday we went to the races again...the weather was very fine and I enjoyed myself exceedingly...on Saturday we had a long walk...on Sunday morning I went to the Cathedral and in the afternoon to St Margaret's Church...William (cousin) drove me home...'

In 1845 Anne spent 5 months staying with Mr and Mrs Atlay, a Beale family connection, at Stamford and then at Fotheringay. '...I nearly always accompanied him when he visited his patients...'[133] Perhaps this was a preparation for her future life.

Anne married at Selling in 1846 Thomas Graham, '...a gentleman of the medical profession... after everything was agreeably settled by a visit of his parents to Kent...' The wedding breakfast was attended by the close family but in the evening there was a large Quadrille Party at Selling. For the honeymoon ...'we went to Southampton the first day after a long journey and arrived at 10pm...the next day we went in a sailing boat to see the ruins of Netley Abbey, a most beautiful place...at 2 pm we went in a steamer boat to Ryde where we stayed a week visiting the most remarkable and prettiest places...one day we walked 12 miles the country was so pretty...for the next week we hired a carriage and made a tour of the Isle of Wight...riding about 25 miles each day...we sailed around the Needles and saw the grand neck...a rock projecting 250 feet over the sea... we saw several caverns in the rocks called Lord Holmes Parlour and another his kitchen, on account of his fondness for lunching on the beach...another cavern is called Frenchman's Hole, where a shipwrecked man was found...when we left we went to Portsmouth and then to Gosport, both of which are very dirty places...then we returned to Holloway...'[134]

Life as the wife of a north London doctor, albeit at that time on the suburban edge of countryside, was very different from that in rural Kent. She commented in 1846 ...'I am agreeably surprised in the house...it is much more comfortable than I expected, my bedroom particularly so, being very nicely furnished and a nice large room...there is a front and a large back garden, with green fields beyond.. but it is very different in the country where things do not get as dirty...' ...' Mr G is very much engaged in his profession...I do not mean to ask him to go anywhere before Christmas, then only for three days to Sole Street...there is so much illness in London...we had to have a fast day yesterday throughout Islington and Holloway...all the shops were closed and only the doctors were working...my husband is very busy and scarcely has time for a meal...he is now a medical visitor with 5 guineas a week but he does not have to put up any medicines, just write prescriptions and the Board of Health pays the chemist...'[135] In 1849 her aunt Curteis wrote...'Mr Graham is getting on in his business well now but it takes a long time for a doctor to get a good practice...they are both so deserving..'[1360]

However, the correspondence with grandmother Beale shows that life was made social by frequent visiting and having relatives to stay. ...'we have a great many visitors and my time seems quite occupied in returning calls...'...yesterday week the trio from Gordon Place dined here and on Thursday we dined there...' ...mama and Mr Hilton paid us a visit last week...they came on Monday when we had a few friends to dinner..on Tuesday we went to ?..on Wednesday we went to St Pauls Churchyard and Ludgate Hill...on Thursday we went again to ?..and Miss Sidebotham[137] dined with us...what delightful weather we have had, I have spent five days at Pinner with Mr and Mrs Graham as Fanny my sister is staying...there were two evening parties there...'[138] In June 1846 she spent a few days at Luton, the Selling home of her spinster aunt.[139] In October 1849 she and her mother were at Walmer. In August 1850 they were at Margate.

By 1851 Anne and Thomas lived at 2 Esther Place, Upper Holloway, Islington.[140] By 1861 they were at 2 Oxford Terrace, Holloway, Islington,[141] and here they remained until the 1880s. They had no children. Thomas who died in 1904 left a sizable personal estate of £19,000.[142]

Fanny Beale Neame, the next surviving child, was born in 1827. She was sent away to school at Norton Street, Marylebone, where in 1841 there was the governess, Miss Mary Sidebotham, two teachers, Miss Williams and Miss Howard, and 12 pupils.[143] In June 1841 she stated...'I came home from school last Thursday accompanied by Aunt Curteis and cousin Elizabeth (who lived in London)...'[144] Her surviving correspondence also gives an insight into Neame home life.

On June 25 1841 she wrote...'Mama, aunt Curteis and Anne are gone to Sittingbourne to meet uncle William Beale on business...they were going in the chaise but as it was so very wet they were obliged to have a fly...we went yesterday to Boughton to see the pottery, where they make crocks, flower pots etc...mama, aunt and I will come to Elmstone (Uncle Richard at Biddenden) next Monday but you must not expect us unless it is a very fine day...if it is wet we will come on Tuesday but if still wet we will not come as we must be home for Thursday...on Tuesday we drank tea with aunt Kate (Neame)...'[145] On 12 December 1846 she reported...'the scarlet fever is raging about very much in this neighbourhood...Mrs Munn[146] has lost two of her children and the baby is now lying very ill with it...Mr and Mrs Graham are coming down and we hope she will remain for three weeks...Elizabeth and I are going to Tenterden on 29th so perhaps we may see you...'[147] On 21 February 1848 she wrote...'Mr and Mrs Ridley,[148] their two babies and the two nurses have been staying with us at Sole Street, Selling for a week...I miss the children so much as I am so fond of playing with them...one of uncle George Neame's daughters died this morning of smallpox...she was only 21 and married a week before Anne...the donkey was so troublesome going home from you...it would only go one foot pace at a time so it took us two and a half hours from Biddenden to Tenterden....'[149]

Fanny Neame married John Lawrence Graham at Selling in 1853. He was the brother of Thomas, and like him was brought up and lived most of his life in London. They set up house at 15 Highbury Grove Villas in Islington and about 1865 moved out to Nower Hill in Pinner. John went into the Civil Service and spent his career in the solicitors department of the Customs Office. They had eight children but only one of those, Annie Jane, had any descendants. John died in 1922 at Broadstairs and left a personal estate of £4,000.[150] One of their sons, Charles Lawrence Graham, was employed as a brewer at Shepherd Neame.

Richard Beale Neame, the third surviving child and eldest son, was born in 1828. Nothing is known about his upbringing nor where he went to school. In 1841 he was at home at Homestall Farm and in 1851, after his widowed mother had remarried, he was living at her new home,

Sole Street House, Selling. Like all his siblings he was close to the Beale relations. In December 1849 he, his Graham sister, his mother and step father, John Neame's youngest son and his friends were all in London staying with the Curteis aunt and uncle. In 1851 his Curteis cousin, Elizabeth, remembered his birthday and then reported to her grandmother that Richard was at Islington with his Graham sister.[151]

As a young man he enjoyed shooting. He was with his Beale uncles at Biddenden in September 1847 and again in 1848, when he invited himself to stay with grandmother Beale. 'I thought I would have a little sport and have a shot at the feathered tribe'. In 1849 he went over to Biddenden again...'to be in readiness for 1st September...I shall bring my dog..I hope will turn out better than the one last year...tell uncle George to have his certificate all ready...I am a famous shot and shall level every bird... your visitors must stay and make off with the game as your larder will be plentifully supplied.'[152]

Richard was the only son to remain in farming. He learnt the business on both his mothers farm and his step father's farm. In 1841 one of his bantams had three young ones.[153] Aged 21 he was writing that ...'we shall have finished harvesting on Thursday weather permitting...we ought to be grateful for the grand crops and the good weather we have had to house them '...In 1848 he wanted to see uncle Pilcher about a bailiff for Homestall.[154] In 1849 his mother wrote...'I must give up going to balls as we get no profits from farming...indeed I fear we shall lose what we have saved...'[155] In 1850 she wrote '...free trade is against farmers saving anything now...I hope we shall be able to keep ourselves...'[156] and his aunt Fanny wrote that '...all farmers are doing badly...'[157]

He took over the tenancy of Homestall and Ewell Farms about 1855. These had been his father's farms, but were retained by his mother and her new husband until he could make a decision about their future. This was at a time when returns had not been propitious but were about to improve steeply. By 1861 he was tenant farming 511 acres in Faversham and Graveney and employed 9 labourers and 3 boys. In 1871 he was described as a farmer and hop farmer.[158] In 1874 he paid a rent of £489 to the Sondes Estate.[159] By 1881 he was employing 25 men and 3 boys for the same acreage.

In 1849 his mother wrote '...he hopes to have a wife with plenty of money...if he can find one... he does not try his luck until he can keep one...'[160] Only in 1859 did he marry; Fanny Stone the only daughter of his neighbour at Goodnestone, near Faversham. Of their five children the two elder sons, Percy Stuart and Austin Beale Neame, took over the tenancy of Homestall Farm from their father in the 1880s but were gone by 1901. The youngest son, Henry Fitzroy Neame, became a fruit farmer at Woodnesborough by 1901.[161] Despite enjoying some very profitable years, followed by the late nineteenth century agricultural depression, Richard died at Hastings in 1893 and left a modest estate of £5,300.[162] None of his children left even that much. His eldest grandson, Richard Stuart Neame, was killed in 1918, at the end of the Great War, aged 19. Richard's line of the family died out in 1940 in ever reducing circumstances.

Elizabeth Beale Neame, the fourth surviving child, was born in 1829. By 1844 she was at the small school at 73 Upper Norton Street her older sister had attended. Like all her family she was a letter writer to her grandmother, relating family and personal events. She relates receiving a cake and oranges from aunt Curteis for her birthday, enjoying her holidays at Sole Street but comments that it is a long time since she heard from home '...and there is a little excuse from mama as she has not been at all well...'[163] In 1846 Mr Hilton gave her a gold watch '...really he is so very considerate and attentive to mamma...' In 1849 she wrote '...have you used your tea trays yet and how do you like them that I found at the Dutch Fair at Biddenden...'[164]

By 1850 family news was of her impending marriage to Mr Mares. In January '...she was busy with her house...' but then in February the wedding was delayed due to the death of her step nieces the Hilton/Munn girls.[165] In June '...the wedding at Sole Street, Selling, was managed very nicely...and the husband often here on family business...'[166]

It was this marriage which ultimately brought The Shepherd Brewery into the Neame family. John Henry Mares came to Faversham and became the joint partner of Henry Shepherd junior, at The Brewery, lately called Shepherd and Hilton but renamed Shepherd and Mares, in 1848. He was born in Maidstone in 1816 and his father was a chemist and druggist at Boxley. How Mares was introduced to the brewery is conjectural; but in the will of his father an executor was Robert Tassell, a relative of James Tassell, who in 1842 had become a partner of Julius Gaborian Shepherd, the family solicitor and first cousin of Henry Shepherd junior. Mares was also a chemist, so with scientific curiosity he probably appealed to the equally interested Shepherd.

His greater asset, however, was his ability to buy out the previous partner, Charles Jones Hilton in cash. What he had to pay is unknown as no partnership deed has survived. Assuming that he paid 50% of the net assets, which were £15,300 inclusive of 'goodwill' which equalled three years profits, he would have had to raise at least £7,650. For a young bachelor of 32 to raise such an amount, and there is no evidence of how he did so, showed considerable self confidence and optimism for the future. At least part of that outlay would have been offset by his marriage settlement in 1850 of probably £3,000.[167] The remainder he would have paid off from future profits and Mares inheritances. This proved to be a good investment, for when he died in 1864 his personal estate totalled £30,000, of which £18,311 was capital in The Brewery.

The Mares moved into a house in East Street, Faversham,[168] but by 1861 they had moved into The Brewery house at 18 Court Street, where they remained until 1864. They appear to have lived a private and modest life 'over the shop'. Mares held only two public offices in Faversham, that of Trustee of the Faversham Public Charities, from 1862, and churchwarden in 1859. They had four daughters, none of whom married farmers or brewers. Elizabeth moved from Faversham when she was widowed and remarried a Surrey doctor, Charles Payne Tomkins. She died in 1893[169] but two daughters remained substantial mortgagees of The Brewery until 1913.

The next sibling, and fifth surviving child, was Austen Beale Neame, who was born at Homestall in 1834. The first reference to his life there is in June 1841, when his mother bought him and his brother Percy a donkey...'mama has bought a donkey for the two little ones to ride on and they have fine fun with that poor thing...I should not like to be it although it has a much better place than before it used to work very hard...'[170]

Like his brothers and sisters he was sent away to school. By 1846 he and Percy were at Hanwell House, Cowley, near Acton in west London, a school run by an Anglican clergyman with about 75 pupils. It was also the school which John, Frederick and Arthur Graham had all attended.[171] Their mother described them as '...well, happy and such good boys at school...'[172] In 1848 their sister Elizabeth reported them as liking their schools very much. In 1849 he '...goes with his master into Nottinghamshire...'[173] Austen left school in 1850.

His family ties with the Grahams and the Beales were close. In 1851 he was living in Islington with his sister and brother-in-law, Thomas and Annie Graham,[174] and was articled to the wholesale grocery firm of his maternal uncle John Curteis, who had only one daughter, partner in Ryde, Curteis and Whitworth, 83 Upper Thames Street, City of London. By 1859 Ryde was dead and in 1862 Austen became a partner in the re-named firm of Curteis Whitworth and Neame. In 1865 they were described as wholesale sugar merchants of 12/13 Eastcheap, London and in 1886 they had offices at 41 Eastcheap and 18 Rood Lane.[175] In his will he was described as a wholesale sugar and dried fruit merchant.

Austen worked in the City and lived in north London all his life. He was a bachelor, with an address at 355 Holloway Road, and he semi-retired to Linton Grange, Fortis Road, Hornsey where he died in 1886. He typified the successful mid Victorian City merchant who left an estate of £45,000.[176] It was bequeathed to charities and the Graham nieces and nephews.

The sixth and youngest child of Austen and Anne Neame was Percy Beale Neame, born in 1836. His father died when he was one so he was brought up by his mother, her close knit extended Beale family, his eldest sisters and in the home of her second husband after 1844, Henry Hilton, at Sole Street, Selling. He must have felt a rather lonely child at times, surrounded by older relations and his older step Hilton brothers and sisters. Perhaps that was so common in the past it was a 'norm'.

He was sent away to school with Austen by 1846, also to Hanwell House, but was soon sent on to a school at Walthamstow, Essex. His sister Elizabeth wrote…'there are about 60 boys and it seems an excellent school. We heard from Percy two days ago and he says he is as happy as he can expect to be and knows half the boys... The summer holiday was spent at Sole Street.[177] In 1847 he was expecting to spend his Michaelmas holidays with his eldest sister Anne Graham in London….he and Austin are very comfortable at their schools…'[178] In February 1849 his mother wrote that …'Austin and Percy are growing into very nice boys…I was sorry to send them back to school as they gave me no trouble at Christmas and agreed so remarkably well.'[179] In December his mother met him at London Bridge; an early use of the railway into East Kent. In 1851 he was still at Walthamstow House.[180]

What he did after leaving school is unknown, but as he became a farmer he probably trained on either the farm of his step father or his elder brother Richard at Homestall. By 1861 he was living at Swanton Lodge, Lydden near Dover and was a bachelor farmer. He employed 8 men and 5 boys with 3 household servants.[181] Most of the land was in the adjoining parish of Swingfield. His choice of both career and the location were strange. Farming had yet to show signs of sustained recovery; Lydden had 'generally poor chalky soil' and Swingfield was a lonely village'.[182] There is no clue as to what drew him away from the Neame traditional territory. Here he remained for about five years, but a gentleman farmer he remained for the rest of his life.

CHAPTER THREE

Percy Neame Brewery Partner 1864-1876

The departure of Percy from farming as his main career is not easy to explain as no correspondence nor family tradition for the period has survived. A number of factors seem to have converged at the same time to bring Percy into brewing and back to Faversham. The catalyst was probably the health of his brother-in-law, John Henry Mares, husband of his sister, Elizabeth. Knowing how close the whole family was this appears to be the most obvious reason; that and the good business opportunities opened up for a young man of 27. The timing was just after the harvest and when his tenancy may have come up for renewal.

The underlying reason for bringing in an additional partner was the death of Henry Shepherd senior in 1862 and the pressing need for his son and executor, Henry Shepherd junior, to pay off or re-arrange the huge mortgage, of £35,000, due to his father's estate. The underlying needs for another partner must have been the growth of the business or the unsuitability or disinterest of the Shepherd brothers.[183] It might also suggest that Henry Shepherd junior was losing interest in the business.

Percy became a partner in the new firm of Shepherd Mares and Neame in October 1864. The arrangement must have been compelling and hurried as no formal transfers of assets and mortgages were made. No co-partnership deeds have survived. Assuming that he became a co-partner for one third of the business Percy would have had to raise £12,000. That equalled one third of the £36,000 net assets of the business, the definition of 'capital in the business' used at that date.[184]

John Henry Mares died on 28 December 1864. Once again the partners had to re-arrange the capital structure of the business. As Mares had no son to contend, Percy Neame became the sole equal co-partner of Henry Shepherd. A resume of the new co-partnership agreement, dated 1 January 1865,[185] has survived. It throws considerable light on the attitude of Henry Shepherd to his old family business. Article 1 recited that the co-partnership shall last 21 years unless determined. Article 5 stated that the capital should belong in equal shares. Article 40 recited that at the death of a partner the other could buy him out subject to a valuation by two 'indifferent persons'.

For this new co-partnership Percy had to raise £18,000 and once again evidence of how he achieved it is lacking. It was an immense sum for a 28 years old youngest son, whose father had died when he was one year old, to raise. There is little explanation of how he achieved it. He inherited only £3,000 from his father.[186] He was as yet unmarried, so he had no capital marriage settlement to invest, and his farming profits, even if he had saved them, would have been modest. His sister, Elizabeth Mares, agreed to leave £10,000, part of the £18,000 capital in the business she had inherited from John Mares, as a mortgage in the Brewery. This would have been a very special arrangement agreed by Henry Shepherd, as a temporary measure until the money could be repaid by Percy from future profits. Such a special arrangement also suggests that without it Mrs Mares may have threatened to put the business up for sale. She clearly deemed her brother Percy was competent enough to protect both the results of her husband's hard work, her family interests and his own. She was paid interest of 5% pa on the loan, double the interest she would have received from Government Stock, but equivalent to the interest her husband received on his 'capital in the business'. Now it was paid out of Percy's 5% interest on his 'capital in the business.'

Assuming that Percy was able to put up £4,000 himself the remaining £4,000 probably came from older Neame or Beale relations in private loans, as the family was very close. This too carried interest of possibly 5%. So, in summary, Percy began his career at the Brewery with personal debts of £14,000 carrying interest charges of £700 pa. His gearing and timing were however perfect.

The business he borrowed (bought) into had been modernised and upgraded once the importance of the railways had been grasped by Shepherd and Mares. The position of The Brewery on the railway junction of Faversham, the dearth of competition from another brewery of size between Canterbury and Chatham, the slowness of Rigden to re-locate his main brewery from Canterbury to Faversham until 1874 were factors in success.

Investment had been widespread and was still in hand in 1864/5. The brew house was rebuilt and re-fitted and new maltings had been built. 'In six years nearly £10,000 of investment was made by the partners.' The product range was widened and advertisements were an innovation to promote new beers and a new image of beer drinking. The Brewery promoted the concept of convenience and reliability for the customers by fixed delivery dates, agencies and stores. Spectacular growth in the numbers of public houses, from 40 to 129, widened outlets, but with discrimination. By 1866 numbers employed at the Brewery had risen to 50.

The result of this was a doubling of output, to 21,323 barrels by 1864, but not of an immediate doubling of turnover or profit. 1866/7 saw turnover rise steeply and from 1868 onwards profits.[187]

As the young new arrival, what did Percy Neame bring to the partnership? It was not a defining amount of cash and it was certainly not experience of brewing or running a business. His expertise was farming, hence knowledge of the qualities and prices of the raw materials of brewing; barley, which was malted, and hops. He would have understood horses, and their provisioning, which for the brewers drays were important throughout his life time. From his family experience Henry Shepherd would have been quite capable in these areas. Percy's understanding of the art of brewing would have been minimal and the running of a public house estate and pricing non-existent. This all gives further credence to the suggestion that the partnership of the 48 years old Henry Shepherd with the 28 years old Percy Neame was forced upon him by Mrs Mares protecting her interests.

Henry Shepherd was always referred to as the senior partner, albeit that he and Percy shared responsibilities. Henry, because of his experience, was for a time the head brewer and concerned with quality control. He was interested in and oversaw the technology of the plant; the furnaces, the new boiler and the quality of coal; the new thermometers and refrigeration plant; the cask cleaning machine and the new railway wagons. He was concerned with employment, advertising and contracts with other brewers. Percy must have been concerned with his own specialisms. Both partners would have agreed pricing and overseen the handling of bad debts. The Letter Book of Henry Shepherd, 1864-1871, does show that he was a diligent businessman.[188] A corresponding Letter Book for Percy has either not survived or his letters were copied into the Letter Book of Henry Shepherd.

It is difficult to prove the division of responsibilities and if there were a driving force. There is no evidence one way or the other, as there was no inter-partner correspondence. In as much as rising successes and returns benefited both partners, then encouraging growth and taking opportunities that were proven, were in their common interests and not contentious. Percy Neame had to learn the business before he could direct policy but as an intelligent young man he would have learnt quickly.

The running of The Brewery estate, of around 100 owned or leasehold public houses, was handled by William Maile, who had joined the business as a solicitors conveyancing clerk by 1857. He was an energetic traveller, by train and horse. He dealt with tenancies, property management, leases, insurances, printing and licenses but not without reference to the partners.[189] He later became the General Manager in all but name. He received a salary of £300 and bonuses that rose from £203 in 1865 to £388 in 1874.[190]

The Neame and Shepherd partnership years were ones of continued expansion and growth, and reaping the full returns of earlier investment.[191] Work continued on improving the buildings on the existing sites and modernising the equipment. In 1865 the new gate secured the yard premises. In 1867/8 the cask washing building and cask shed was built. In 1869 a new tun room and stores were built. The new offices at 17 Court Street were completed in the same year. In 1874 the programme of modernisation was completed with the new Ale Malt and Hop Stores. All these were designed by the Faversham architect Benjamin Adkins and most were built by the Faversham firm of Shrubsole. In all £8,500 was spent on The Brewery and £4,000 to complete Preston Maltings.

A further £7,700 was spent on new equipment. In 1866 Carty erected four new tuns, a mash tun and yeast, liquor and hop backs. Pontifex provided four new temperators and Foulson provided a 35 barrels refrigerator. In 1870 James Seamark, the engineer of West Street, Faversham, installed a new boiler. By 1874 four steam engines '...gave motion to the several appliances used in grinding, mashing, boiling, steaming, cask cleaning and other processes...these developments created one of the most extensive and complete breweries in the country...' In 12 years £30,000 was spent on the brewery. Modernisation on this scale was not repeated for another 25 years.

Production, spurred on by improved mechanisation, increased in these years but not as at the same rate as the Mares years. In 1865/6 The Brewery sent out 30,600 barrels and in 1873/4 it sent out 44,432 barrels; a number not achieved again until the 1920s. This was an increase of 50%. The product range continued to change. In 1864 Mild Beer accounted for 27% of the barrelage, Bitter Beer for 22% and Pale Ale 5%. In 1874 Mild Beer accounted for 27% of barrelage, Bitter Beer for 33% and Pale Ale 15%. In the words of The Faversham Mercury ' ...in recent years the firm have paid particular attention to the brewing of family pale ales and the more delicate beers, the result of which has been so great an extension of their business...' This trend is all the more interesting as it was a shift towards the most expensive beers. Mild Ale was 28/- per barrel, Bitter was 28/- per barrel and Pale Ale was 38/- per barrel. Public taste was changing, at least in East Kent.

Viewed against national trends these production figures were impressive. The population of England increased by only 15% and the national barrelage increased by 25%. The Brewery doubled the national trend.

The continued opening of new stores along the railway lines improved distribution. In 1865 The Brewery leased 4 stores and in the following 10 years it leased a further 5 stores. Sittingbourne and New Brompton came in 1867, Ashford came in 1869 and the London stores at Penge and Camberwell followed in 1870 and 1871. The importance of the trade they did is reflected in their sales figures, although some stores were very modest. Penge looked like something out of the Wild West whereas the Camberwell Stores were under the massive brick arches of the railway lines. Sheerness continued to be the most important store outside Faversham. In 1865 The Brewery or Home Stores accounted for 66% of sales; by 1875 this figure had fallen to 47%. The importance of the railway was summed up in a letter of William Maile dated 14 March 1876 '...as our trade is done principally by railway the subject of turnpike tolls little affects us...'

Horse drawn dray transport continued to be vital however, as the stables accounts show. Barrels were delivered by drays from the Home Stores to the town and adjoining villages. Barrels were taken by drays to Faversham station, where they were loaded onto trucks and despatched and then off loaded at the receiving station onto stores drays. Local deliveries were made by the local stores drays. From 1874 a traction engine with wagon attached served the local villages and Ashford.

With the development of the railways the ownership of railway wagons occupied both Henry Shepherd and William Maile. The Brewery bought its first truck in 1861. In 1865 they applied to put another truck on the line and in 1869 they bought three wagons from the Midland Wagon Company, Birmingham. The truck panels were painted blue and the ironwork was picked out in black. In 1871 two vans were purchased from the Gloucester Wagon Company; the livery was cream base with dark blue lettering with gold shading and the ironwork was black. By 1874 The Brewery operated 10 railway trucks between Dover, Ramsgate and London.

The Brewery sales outlets continued to be the public house and the private household. The most important outlet was the public house. Between 1865 and 1875 the total number of public houses fell from 129 to 98 but this disguises a shift in policy. The number of freehold houses rose from 55 to 59 and the number of leaseholds fell from 74 to 39. The biggest fall was in the Isle of Sheppey where 12 leaseholds were not renewed. In March 1870 a letter from William Maile stated '...property at Sheerness is very un-saleable..due to uncertainty in the Dockyard...' The conclusion of the Crimean War, which had boosted demand, meant the contraction in the number of servicemen stationed there. In Herne Bay 5 leaseholds lapsed, possibly because it had failed to expand as a resort and in Canterbury 3 leases lapsed. The choice of the sitting of public houses was sensitive to the wider economy of the county. Quality of public houses was also a concern, for The Brewery acquired only 2 beer houses in these years; one in West Street, Faversham and one in Sheldwich.

Private sales increased as a percentage of Brewery turnover. In 1858 13% of turnover derived from private sales but by 1866 this had risen to 20%. Advertising promoted the new family and lighter beers to a wider audience. Newspaper advertisements reminded the public weekly, and, for the travelling public, railway station advertisements reminded them daily of Shepherd Neame Pale Ales and Family Bitter. In 1865 The Brewery wanted to put up a board at Bickley Station; in 1874 an advertising board was painted for Farningham Road Station and in March 1870 '...Mr Maile sketched out the lettering we require at Victoria Arches...' In 1870 The Brewery printed 10,000 circulars and cards for distribution at Penge Station. These colourful printed flyers were packed with information. They listed stores, agencies, specialities, stock and prices. They always carried the words '...Orders will receive prompt attention...'

All these increases meant more staff were taken on. In 1861 22 men were employed. By 1871 the staff numbers had trebled to 72 men and boys. By 1874 there were 80 and by 1881 Percy Neame was employing 100 men and boys. By 1875 there were 4 clerks in the office. A modern office structure was emerging.

For The Brewery to have achieved these advances and bucking the national trends, the competition must have been at best ill focused and at worst weak in East Kent. The competing brewery in Faversham, of W E & J Rigden, was only expanded from 1874 when they relocated their main Canterbury operation but even in 1881 they employed only 44 men and boys. None of the 6 breweries in Canterbury employed more than 30 men each. In 1871 Gardiner at Ash employed only 29 men and the breweries in Ashford and Sittingbourne employed no more than 12 men each. Even Ralph Fremlin at Maidstone employed only 76 men and boys in 1871 and 138 in 1881.

These successes translated into strengthened Balance Sheets and improved Profit and Loss Accounts. Between 1866 and 1875/6 the' fixed and current gross assets' grew from £109,000 to £164,000. These were made up of approximately 60% for the freehold and leasehold estate, 20% for stocks and debtors, 10% for plant utensils and casks, 5% for cash at the bank and 4% from 1871 for 'goodwill in the business'. The 'creditors' in 1867 were represented by loans of £58,000, trade of £5,000, interest and profit to the partners of £3,000 which left a 'capital balance' or net assets of £43,000. This the partners deemed their 'capital in the business'. In 1876 the loans had fallen to £50,000 and the 'capital in the business' was £98,000.

In 12 years, from 1864 to 1876, Percy Neame saw his investment grow from £20,000 to £50,000. In addition, during this partnership, he was paid 50% of the net profit. This amounted to £62,000 or £5,000 pa on average. To pay the £700 pa interest charges and repayment instalments on the loans of £14,000 was well within his means. His income, the net profit, also financed a very comfortable private life.

Percy Neame moved in 1865 to The Mount, then still known as Mount Ospringe, on the western edge of Faversham.[192] He probably leased it at first from the executors of General Gosselin. For a young man with all his capital committed to The Brewery it is unlikely he could afford a price of about £1,500. Soon it would have been well within his budget.[193]

The house had been built by Bonnick Lipyeat about 1760 and was inherited ultimately by his daughter who married the General. The early house faced the London Road but this was trebled in size by the Gosselins about 1825 by the addition of the long wing which contained a new sweeping entrance front, more reception rooms, service rooms and many bedrooms.[194] There were about 5 acres of gardens and grounds. The disadvantage was its proximity to both the London Road and the new railway line. Once again one senses Percy found a bargain, especially as the previous tenant of one year had just been declared bankrupt.

The following year Percy married at Selling his first cousin once removed, Florence Neame. She was 19 and he was 29. Her father, Harry Neame, was the second son of John Neame, the uncle of Percy. Harry left Selling to farm at Allans Court, Minster in the Isle of Thanet. Her mother was Mary Anne Collard, the daughter of Henry Collard, of Grays near Chislet, who in 1851 farmed about 1,000 acres.[195] Harry died soon after in 1848 leaving his young widow Mary Anne Neame with the one surviving daughter aged 1. His estate was modest; he was only able to leave £3,000 capital to his wife, on which she received a life income.[196] When Henry Collard died in 1857 Mary Anne did inherit the income for life on 50% of his £9,000 estate. The other half went to her sister, Jane Harrison.[197]

Florence was not the great heiress with whose inheritance her husband bought The Brewery. The only capital she brought to the marriage was £2,000[198] inherited from her grandfather, John Neame of Selling.[199] The capital of her father and maternal grandfather, on which her mother received the income for her life, only came to Florence much later when her mother died in 1900.[200] That was about £7,500.

Upgrading and modernising the house went hand in hand with starting a family. From the evidence surviving canted bay windows were inserted in the west facing reception rooms to capture more light, mouldings and timber frames were replaced and chunky fireplaces inserted.[201] From the design of these it is likely that the local Faversham architect, Benjamin Adkins, who was the brewery architect and surveyor from the 1860s to the 1890s,[202] was responsible. Creating nurseries for children and rooms for a large household staff followed.

Within the first 8 years of marriage 6 children were born; Marion in 1867, Harry Sidney in 1869, Florence in 1870, Arthur in 1871, Alick Percy in 1873 and Ida in 1874. In 1871 the household indoor staff consisted of a cook, a housemaid, a ladies maid, a page and a nurse.[203]

The arrival of his children replaced the losses of his older Neame and Beale relations that had been so important in his youth. In 1875 his mother died at Selling and Percy with his two brothers were the executors. She left the surprisingly large estate of £25,000 to her six children equally. His step father, Henry Hilton, who had died the week before, left £14,000, but to his children from his first marriage.[204]

How Percy occupied his time outside The Brewery is difficult to establish, as no personal records survive. He did not hold any public offices and the dearth of references to him in the local newspapers, those unique recorders of all local activities, suggest that he was a private man working hard and enjoying family life. Limited time was available for any activities outside The Brewery, as Saturday was a normal working day and Sunday morning was taken up by church at Faversham.

In December 1875 his partner, Henry Shepherd, died in London aged 59.[205] There is no evidence that Henry planned for his children to be partners in The Brewery. The opposite is true. As his will drawn up in 1868 makes no mention of the business nor the partnership, this suggests that he was content that the terms of the 1865 Partnership Agreement would operate; Percy could buy out the Shepherd heirs if he so wished.

Henry left 4 sons, none of whom made successes of their lives. One, who married his aunt's parlour maid, was an alcoholic and died penniless under a Portsea tram;[206] one gave up the Bar to become a theatre critic and died penniless; the other two both died young, intestate, and before their mother. Only the youngest Harry Reginald Garrard Shepherd was working in The Brewery and he was dismissed immediately by Percy with salary in lieu of notice.[207]

Mrs Shepherd, and her children, despite having lived her entire life in the town, left Faversham forever and by 1919 this branch of the family was nearly extinct. As the sole executrix she sold the business, sold the contents of 18 Court Street and removed to Eltham to live a comfortable widowhood with her daughter for nearly 20 years. After 11 years learning all aspects of the brewing business Percy Neame was able to become sole proprietor; but that was at a cost.

CHAPTER FOUR

Percy Neame Sole Proprietor 1876-1895

Henry Shepherd died on 22 December 1875 and was buried within the week at Davington. On 13 January 1876 Percy Neame gave notice to Mrs Shepherd that he wished to purchase the 50% share in The Brewery of her late husband. Each party appointed an assessor. Percy appointed William Woodley Mason of 61 King William Street, London, the long standing auditor of The Brewery, as his valuer and arbitrator. Mrs. Shepherd appointed Alfred Thomas of 2 Adelaide Place, London as hers. On 31 October the award was made. Percy Neame was to pay Mrs Shepherd £41,100. Mrs Shepherd refused and queried the articles of the partnership.

On 11 December Percy commenced an Action in Chancery to seek specific performance. On 23 January 1877 Mrs Shepherd delivered her defence. Soon after both agreed that the action be stayed. The Order of Court was made on 5 May 1877 wherby Percy agreed to pay Mrs Shepherd an additional £2,250. This enormous amount he agreed to pay into court. The sureties for an £80,000 bond that he had to deliver were his brother-in-law, Thomas Graham, and his first cousin, Edward Neame of Selling Court.[208] The bond was to be void if the balances were paid by 22 December 1878. In six lengthy conveyances of July 1877 the entire brewery business, estate, mortgages, stock, utensils, cash, debts and their miscellaneous shares in the Faversham Gas and Cattle Market Companies were transferred by Mrs Shepherd to Percy Neame.[209]

Once again the question arises of where Percy raised £43,350, an enormous amount of money. £16,000 he raised from his own resources and from his closest family as no record of this is contained in the Private Ledger. From the recent death of his mother he inherited £4,500, from his marriage settlement he received £2,000 and if his mother-in-law agreed to invest her capital,

31

already settled on her daughter Florence at her death, that released a further £7,500.[210] The remaining £2,000 probably came from Percy.

Percy showed a financial acuteness in raising the remaining capital of £27,350 he needed. He used the security of the bond from his relations to negotiate very short term loans. From Mrs Shepherd he obtained a short term allowance of £13,400 and he borrowed the remainder. He borrowed £10,200 from the family of his general manager, William Maile, and £3,700 from a number of local people.[211] Their security was the bond but when the business was conveyed Percy converted their loans immediately into mortgages, which were added to the existing mortgages and loans secured on The Brewery.

Buying The Brewery by raising mortgages on its assets to do so was not new. Henry Shepherd and Charles Hilton had done just that in 1844. They had borrowed on mortgage £40,000 from Henry Shepherd senior to secure the business.[212] Once Percy was the sole proprietor of The Brewery all its assets were his personal property to use as he wished.

Having secured a business that had been expanded and whose plant had been totally modernised, Percy firstly consolidated his balance sheet in the years 1878 to 1880 and thereafter increasingly improved it. He built steadily upon what he had purchased. Here was Percy the investor, his first and primary role in the business.

In 1875 the net asset value (defined as Capital Balance in the Balance Books) of The Brewery was £91,690 which fell to £71,570 in 1878, due to the additional purchase mortgages. By 1880 it recovered to £87,837 and by 1885 it rose to £112,000. By 1890 it had risen to £132,829 and by 1895 the net asset value of the business had nudged up to £135,572. In 17 years from the nadir of 1878 to 1895 the net value of the business had increased by 90% or a little over 5% per annum.

This was achieved by Percy in his second role as Chief Executive of the business. His strategy was to reduce debt but at the same time increase investment; and that meant investment in the main sales outlet and asset of the brewery, the freehold and leasehold estate.

In 1875 the mortgages totalled £50,408 then they rose to £77,469 by 1878, to finance the purchase of the business. By 1885 mortgages had dropped to £63,074 and by 1895 they had dropped further to £59,359. In the 17 years from 1878 to 1895 they had fallen by 25% whilst the net value of the business had risen by 90%.

The mortgagees fell into two groups; family members and key employees or other locals. The former were more akin to shareholders and the later commercial lenders.

Throughout these years the Mares family continued to hold their investment, dating back to 1848, through their mortgages in The Brewery. This fluctuated from the original £18,300 held by Percy's sister Mrs Mares, later Mrs Tomkins, and her daughter Mrs Boddington, in 1878; to £17,300 in 1890, held by Mares executors and his daughters Mrs Boddington, Mrs Gurrey and Mrs Woodruff and Mrs Mares; and down to £9,000 held by the Boddington and Gurrey Trustees in 1895. By 1890 further members of the family of Percy Neame held mortgages. His brother, Richard Beale Neame, held £4,900, his nephew, Henry Fitzroy Neame held £2,026, his brother-in-law Thomas Graham held £3,800 and other Neame Trustees held £2,840. By 1895 the reducing Mares mortgages were replaced by those of Graham and Neame family members. In 1878 only 24% of the mortgages were held by family but by 1895 44% of mortgages were held by Percy's relations. The business was effectively held by a tight family circle, which, as far as financial management was concerned, ensured continuity and certainty for Percy the owner.

Other reliable mortgagees were the Maile family. In 1878 they held 13% of the mortgages but by 1885 they held £13,000 of mortgages or 21% of the total. With the death of William in 1885 and the withdrawal of his son from the business their share had reduced to a mere 6% by 1895.

Mid way between the associated and the commercial mortgagees were the Tassells, who were directly descended from James Shepherd, a younger son of Julius Shepherd.[213] Whilst being members of the extended Shepherd family they remained not only solicitors of The Brewery, until the 1960s, but had substantial client funds to invest. In 1880 they had £5,000 on mortgage to The Brewery; by 1895 they had mortgages of £20, 000 with The Brewery. With 34% of the total mortgages, they were the biggest creditors of the firm.

At the other end of the spectrum were the commercial mortgagees. The main one in 1878, no doubt out of short term necessity for Percy Neame, was Mrs Shepherd who held £13,400. This was paid off by 1880. The £10,500 remaining of the old 1844 Henry Shepherd senior mortgage, later held by his executors, remained until paid off in 1883. In 1880 the first purely commercial mortgage of £6,000 came from the Hilton Rigden Bank. This rose to £10,000 by 1890 but had been repaid by 1895. To be beholden to the family of brewing bankers who were competitors on the other side of the street cannot have been a comfortable arrangement, but even they understood a sound investment. The balance of the mortgages were held by locals such as Higham the printer, Mrs Shaw, Mr Hadley, the Cullens, Mr Coe and Masons the London auditors.[214]

What distinguished all these mortgages was that the collateral was real estate, so the investments were at virtually nil risk. That came with the commensurately low interest return of 2 1/2% per annum.

Percy paid great attention to the development of his real estate. This was in his third role as Estates Director. Between 1878 and 1885 the value, taken at cost, rose from £95,000 to £108,000. By 1895 it was valued at £136,000. Over 17 years his investment in his public house estate was

£41,000. Cumulatively this was 42% or approximately 2 1/2% per annum. His strategy was the improvement of both the quality and the location of the houses.

Between 1878 and 1885 the total numbers fell, from 98 houses to 94 houses, but the fall disguises a substantial shift in type and location. [Tables 3 & 4. Shepherd Neame Public Houses. 1865-1913] In 1878 there were 59 freehold houses; in 1885 there were 69 freeholds and a reduced number of 25 leasehold houses. Moreover, there were changes in location. In the Isle of Sheppey, always dependent upon the dockyard and hence war economies, 10 leaseholds were reduced to 5 and 2 pubs were purchased freehold. In the towns the numbers of pubs doubled from 7 to 14. The numbers of pubs in Faversham and the villages remained static. The numbers of leasehold pubs spread along the London Road halved; an interesting reflection on the transfer of general trade from the road to the railway.

The purchase of a freehold estate in Whitstable was a new departure. The Coach and Horses, the East Kent Hotel, the Four Horseshoes, the Duke of Cumberland and the Rising Sun were added in these years.

Between 1885 and 1895 the estate was further increased. In 1895 it consisted of 106 houses of which 82 were freehold and 24 leasehold. The shift towards freehold houses continued. The purchases were spread across all locations. They included the Cherry Tree at Preston next Faversham, the Dove at Dargate, the Gate at Marshside and the Greyhound at Rochester, which was the first acquisition in that city. Only in the villages were new leaseholds purchased; the Griffins Head at Chillenden, the Palm Tree at Elham, the Rose and Forge at Kennington, the Acorn at Birchington, the George at Leeds, the Unicorn at Bekesbourne and the Lord Nelson at Waltham. These substitute leaseholds, which could be cancelled easily, were outside The Brewery hinterland and were probably a test of new markets without the bigger outlay of freeholds.

Improvements to existing and new pubs were made constantly.[215] Between 1876 and 1895 the annual general expenditure was between £1,600 and £2,000. In addition specific works were carried out. For example in 1877 a new club room, an especially popular addition to pubs at that time, was added to the Plough and Harrow at Bridge for £162 and a further £400 spent on a general upgrade. In 1879 £400 was spent on additions to the Four Horseshoes. In 1880 E Fuller, builder of Faversham, made improvements to the Bell at Sittingbourne. In 1884 £250 was spent on additions to the George at Newnham. In 1888 the Fishermans Arms at Whitstable were rebuilt by Foad for £303. In 1890 additions to the Bear at Faversham were carried out by Whitings the Faversham builder for £300 and new stables were built for The East Kent for £119. In 1893 H. Hogben built a new stable at the Railway Hotel, Faversham; a reminder of how important stabling was for railway companies and related hotels.

The trade generated by the public houses varied greatly.[216] In Faversham the Royal William, which was new built in 1865 as the main public house on the new 'Cooksditch Estate', in St Mary's Road, and which had a popular club room for large local social functions, had a turnover of around 480 barrels per annum during the period. The Railway Hotel, opposite Faversham Railway Station, had a turnover of about 430 barrels per annum, which fell erratically during the period. The St Anne's Cross, close to the Faversham Gunpowder Works and Tannery, had a turnover of 312 barrels per annum which rose steadily. By comparison the Sun in West Street had a turnover of 230 barrels which fell slightly during the period. The Bear in Market Place maintained a turnover of 200 barrels per annum. Further down the scale were the Shakespeare in West Street, the Anchor in Abbey Street, the Three Tuns in Tanners Street and the Castle in West Street whose trade was about 180 barrels per annum and falling.

On the London Road at Sittingbourne the Fountain had a turnover of 400 barrels per annum, the Globe and Engine a turnover of 320 barrels per annum and the Milton Arms a turnover of 285 barrels per annum. The Chequers at Lenham, for a reason difficult to discover, had the highest turnover of all for a time at 572 barrels per annum. Lower down the scale country pubs like the Three Mariners at Oare had a turnover of 286 barrels per annum and the Sondes Arms at Selling a turnover of 180 barrels per annum.

Just as investment was made in the pub estate so was investment made in The Brewery site. In 1879 the Wharf, adjacent to Bridge Street, which gave The Brewery more direct access to the Creek, was purchased from H & J Barnes for £1,100. In 1880 unspecified Brewery improvements costing £400 were made. In 1888 the leading Faversham builders, R M & H Whiting, built new stores at Mill Row for £695. In 1895 The Brewery purchased the old bakers shop adjoining the office, 16 Court Street, from Isaac Dan the wine merchant for £500. Incremental improvements, took the business forwards.

The scale of investment in the plant and utensils was very modest when compared to the fundamental modernisation carried out in the mid 1860s. Between 1876 and 1895 barely £600 a year was spent here; little more than maintenance expenditure.[217]

With the coming of the railway, and later the traction engines, the building and leasing of Brewery stores became increasingly viable. Large quantities of stock could be moved quickly and cheaply to depots 30 or 50 miles from The Brewery. From them stock was sold on to public houses, agencies and local customers. Local horse drawn drays made the deliveries.

Distribution of stock was through the network of stores spread through Kent and outer London, all of which were well established by 1880. The main store was at The Brewery in Faversham. Within twenty miles stores were at, in descending order of stock traded, Sheerness, Ashford,

of the day as interest on capital 'lent' to a business by its partners. This practice was established at The Brewery in 1866, just after his arrival, by Percy and Henry Shepherd.[231] In addition Percy paid himself the net profit of the business. This did fluctuate from £12,900 in 1878, to a nadir of £4,632 in 1890 and to a partial recovery to £8,337 in 1895. The average profit Percy paid himself was a little over 5% of the net assets. This profit is after the deduction of £2,300 per annum on average for capital investment on new freeholds and the average annual repayment of debt of £1,200, which is not dissimilar from the average amounts spent in the years of 1858-1867 on 'strengthening the balance sheet'.[232] [Table 2]. However, compared to the average net profit for 1867 to 1877 of 12% plus 5% interest per annum these figures illustrate once again the decline in net returns. In part compensation he paid himself a salary of £700 per annum from 1891.[233]

From 1877 to 1885 Percy relied substantially on William Maile as the Brewery General Manager. He dealt with tenants, tenancies, property management, leases, insurances, licensing, advertising, printing and the day to day supply of houses. He was constantly travelling around Kent and up to London, which was made easier by the railway connections.[234] He was remunerated by a basic salary of £500 per annum to which was added a commission on profits of 3 1/2%, which was fixed at £300 per annum as profits fell. To this was added the miscellaneous fees he was paid for his semi private work of conveyancing for The Brewery. Without his reliability the business would have needed another partner.

Below William Maile was a small office staff of clerks who handled routine correspondence, administration and accounts.[235] In 1877 there were possibly 7; S Hills, GE Boorman, J Veitch, W Boorman, W Veitch, Matson and Attwater. Their salaries ranged from £150 to £60 per annum supplemented by an annual 'donation' or bonus from Percy at his discretion.[236] This ranged from £50 for Hills, Boorman and Veitch to £15 for W Boorman. By 1885 the numbers had grown by the addition of William E D Maile, the son of William. He was paid a salary of £250 per annum, higher than that of any of the other clerks. By 1894 the numbers had reduced again to 6, with the departure of Maile junior for a wine merchant in Dedham, Suffolk. The selection of these clerks depended directly on Percy, to whom they were directly responsible. Here he was in the role of Personnel Director.

The brew house had its own little hierarchy directly responsible to Percy in his role of Director of Brewing. As there is no evidence of a head brewer in these years he was probably the active brewer. In 1879 he took on his nephew, Charles Lawrence Graham, the third son of his sister, Fanny and his brother in law, John Lawrence Graham, aged 19. He was trained as a brewer and by 1887 had probably become the senior brewer as he was paid the substantial salary of £350 per annum.[237] He remained at The Brewery until his death in 1930.[238] In the same year Percy took on Holliday and Wilkinson as trainee/assistant brewers, with salaries of £82 and £90 per annum respectively.

Within The Brewery was a substantial staff of store keepers, draymen, stable men and general labourers. In addition were the maltsters with their assistants and labourers working at the three Faversham malt houses. The names of virtually none of them have survived. Beyond The Brewery at each of the 10 stores was a store keeper, at least one clerk, one draymen and a labourer.

In 1881 Percy employed 100 men and boys.[239] This suggests that if 7 were clerks, 3 were brewing assistants, 15 were employed malting, 50 were employed at the stores, then about 25 general brewery workers were employed at The Brewery.

As well as the production roles of Percy Neame were his supply roles. He was Director of Procurement, a role which as a farmer he understood and probably enjoyed most. He must have been in his element sampling, negotiating and choosing barley and hops, the primary ingredients of his beer.[240]

These were the main expenses of brewing. The average expenditure per annum on barley was £16,500 and on hops £7,000. The annual expenses fluctuated in accordance with the market and especially the season. The variations in barley prices were far less than those of the temperamental hop production. For barley they were between £26,047 in 1879 and £9,319 in 1889. In 1883 Percy spent the highest amount ever on hops of £17,626 and in 1879 the lowest of only £825.

All the barley came from East Kent sources and was malted at the three Brewery malt houses; the Home, within The Brewery site; The Preston by Faversham Station; and The Standard Malthouse in Abbey Street near Faversham Creek. The Brewery malted virtually all the barley it needed. The Home was the smallest and on a very restricted old site. The Preston was built as new in 1866 and The Standard had been extended some years previously. If 1899 is a guide to sourcing ten years earlier, approximately 20% of the barley came from farmers in Birchington and the remainder came from farms within 5 miles of Faversham. In 1893 barley came from 12 farmers in Thanet; F Collard, C Mascall, J Stannard, E Orpin, C Hunter, D Williams, W Smith, E Maxted junr', Studhams, W Barling, G R Chase and F Mayhew.[241]

The hops, like the barley, came from East Kent sources and from farms especially close to Faversham. On 30th September 1880 the stocks recorded totalled 837 pockets or 1189 cwts. from 10 growers. Of those 352 pockets came from Percy's elder brother Richard Beale Neame who was still farming at Homestall Farm, Faversham; 113 pockets came from his cousin E B Neame farming at Selling; 95 pockets came from Frank Bridge Cobb, the son in law of William Maile, farming at Town Place, Throwley; 55 pockets came from another cousin E Neame at Selling; and the remainder came from T Monk, J Sladden, W Perkins and A Curling.

In 1885 the stock recorded totalled 1249 pockets and came from a larger number of 22 growers The biggest supplier was Frank Bridge Cobb with 239 pockets; followed by E Neame with 205 pockets. T Powell supplied 119 pockets and Peckham 86 pockets. R B Neame supplied 80 pockets. The prices varied. E Neame was paid the maximum of £9.9.0 a pocket, for 25 pockets and J. Jones the minimum of £6 a pocket for a mere 7 pockets. The biggest growers were paid between £7.10.0 and £8 per pocket.

In 1890 the stock recorded totalled 869 pockets. The biggest supplier was T Powell with 380 pockets. The next were Percy Stuart Neame and his brother Austin Beale Neame, the eldest sons of Richard Beale Neame, the brother of Percy, who had taken over their fathers farm at Homestall; they supplied 165 pockets. James French supplied 63 pockets and Henry Minter 61. The prices varied between a maximum of £5.5.0 for Mr Powell's hops down to £4 a pocket for some of the hops of Percy's nephews. By 1895 only 403 pockets were recorded of which 198 came from T Powell and 43 pockets from Homestall. The price was £4.4.0 or 4 guineas. The falling prices of the hops is noticeable.

The situation was well summarised in a letter from George Boorman dated 3 October 1893. "Faversham is in the midst of the most celebrated hop gardens and the finest barley growing district of East Kent...so we can select direct from growers..."[242]

As sole proprietor of The Brewery, Percy's active and daily involvement in every aspect of the business was needed if he were to protect his investments and the interests of his family. He was a significant letter writer on all subjects of management as the General Out Letter Books illustrate. He was no mere figurehead drawing profits without commitment. His daily rounds of tasks derived directly from each of his executive roles. With the exception of Sundays he was at The Brewery or travelling to business meetings every day of the week. In January 1886 he wrote '... I cannot get away from The Brewery as often as I wish...I have engaged Mr Veitch and the son of the late Mr Maile to do the travelling...'[243] By 1893 Mr Boorman was an additional traveller.[244] In November 1886 Maile wrote '...Mr Neame will be at The Brewery every day this week from 10am...'

For one or more days each week Percy was visiting the houses, stores, suppliers or in London. For example in April 1894 he was at Eastling, Hernhill, the Dove at Dargate, the Dolphin at Boughton, the Brunswick Arms at Teynham and the George at Elmstead. In May he was in London to meet amongst others the coal merchant, Mr Morgan.[245]

Selecting good public house tenants, the ultimate source of his income, and sanctioning bad ones, absorbed a lot of his time. His attitudes come through in so many of his letters to them. In May 1891 he wrote to Mr Collard '... your groom James Anderson has applied for a house at

Borden that I have just purchased...I am pleased for him to remain with you until you replace him...meanwhile I will put in one of our men we frequently send out to take the management waiting...'[246]

Debt was a common problem. In May 1886 he wrote to one...'you have not paid anything of rent... make good your promises or I will put an end to your tenancy...'[247] To ten he wrote reminding them of outstanding accounts in May 1887.[248] 'The account is enclosed....you really must pay more often...what if all my tenants owed me this large amount...' On 23 November 1888 he wrote '...the only way to save you from ruin is for you to pay over the amount demanded...you had better come to see me Monday next...' To another the following week he wrote...'I do not wish for any further delay in your affairs...you must come to the Brewery on Friday next...'

Some private clients were equally indebted to Percy. In February 1887 Percy wrote to Rev. Kingsford of Newnham reminding him that three years accounts were outstanding. '...please save me the unpleasantness of taking steps...'

After debt was concern about behaviour. In July 1890 he wrote to the tenant of the Globe and Engine at Sittingbourne '...Dear Madam, When I accepted you as a tenant it was on the understanding that certain partiers were not to be entertained on the premises...that is not adhered to...should that continue I will have to find another tenant.' In the following month he wrote again '...should I hear any more I shall give notice to quit...I trust for the sake of your family you will not force me.' A similar letter went out in October 1890 to Mr M J Martin. '...you must be more careful not to serve any that have had too much to drink...do not allow females to hang about the house...get rid of all tough characters...'[249] Damage to reputation was always a concern. Percy summed that up in March 1893 '...much harm it has done us...it is easy to lose a good name but difficult to get it back...' In October 1891 he wrote to Mr Cheeseman saying '... sorry to hear of men getting drunk on your premises at day time and becoming unfit for work... you must be more careful...magistrates are very particular about licences...'

Praise of tenants by Percy was as common as reprimand. In June 1891 he wrote of John Filmer seeking a reference '...he conducted our house very well...he would make a good tenant...' In January 1892 Mr Maile wrote '..Mr Neame does not refuse tenancies to widows if they wish to carry on the business...'[250] In July 1894 he wrote to Edward Hogben at the Ship 'I thank you and your father for the trade of so many years...'[251] Perhaps the overview of Percy was summarised in a letter of September 1885. ' We have not found at present that public houses are the mine of gold represented.'[252]

Concern for product quality, by acting immediately and answering complaints immediately, was also good management. Bad handling as well as the vagaries of the weather had much to answer for. In July 1885 Percy wrote '...many bad casks from Sheerness Stores through being improperly corked and bunged...' In August 1890 Percy wrote to Mr Humphreys '...I am sorry we cannot send ale you like...I tried one this morning and it was very good...of course it takes a few days for it to become bright after travel and unless it is so it never will be nice...'[253] In November 1891 Mr Maile wrote '...sorry for the complaint...the electrical state of the atmosphere interfered with some brewings...our store keeper at Canterbury will deliver you more...'[254] In October 1893 Percy wrote to Rev Bloomfield at Hythe '...The brewing for October in our Ashford Stores is not in sound condition due to the exceptionally hot weather this summer.'

Choice of ingredients and materials also concerned Percy. He was interested in the quality and price of coals. In April 1895 he wrote to F W Morgan and Co. in London '...we are now about to buy our coals for malting...please quote your price for the usual quality of years past...'[255] He had complete control over the selection of both barley for malting and hops. He clearly had a discriminating nose. In December 1885 he wrote '...I am in receipt of a further letter about Hope's barley...I was most particular about enquiring on which farm it was grown...I now feel much aggrieved about the whole transaction...'[256] In the same month he wrote to Mr J Wood. '...I have received 40qtrs of the Cowstead barley...it is very irregular in quality...there are only 54lbs per bushel when weighed...not worth it...in fact not good enough...ask you bailiff to give me particulars...' In the next month he wrote '...I can give you 36/- for the barley. The fodder had rather too much trefoil in it'.

In respect to hops Percy wrote to one grower in 1889 that '...we are not in want of hops...large stock but send samples...we may take a few.' To Mr Newman he wrote '...we have looked at your hops but they are very indifferent and want using at once...I offer £2 per pocket...'[257] In 1891 he wrote to Mr Cornes at Willesborough that he did not consider 1890 hops with anything but the price now. To Mr Goodhew in 1894 he wrote a cheery letter '...your hops are of little use... they are very bad indeed...I doubt if you will find anyone to buy them...I wish you a happy and prosperous New Year.'[258]

Pricing of the products was the ultimate decision of Percy. In July 1889 he wrote '...we cannot supply beer cheaper than our Table Beer...except at harvest time when we brew a cheaper beer for the neighbourhood...'[259] In January 1888 he was rattled at one complaint from Mr F R Hartley and replied '...we are astonished at the contents of your letter after so many years we have had no complaints...we will not reduce our prices...as we have many applications for our beer...'[260]

Percy's letters make some references to his employees. The men in the yard were allowed 3 pints of beer a day. He was happy to employ sons of old employees. Reprimands for carelessness were rare. However, in 1886 two men '...Taylor and Theobalds were sent to Lenham where they ought to have led their horses by a cart...instead they drove them...the accident ought never to have happened...I have given them notice to leave next week although they have been with us some time...such carelessness must be stopped...I will have the expenses of the accident...'[261]

Investment opportunities, outside The Brewery, were largely ignored by Percy. In 1885 he wrote to a Mr Hollands that '...we do not intend to take any debentures as we have plenty of employment for our capital...'

In these years there were a number of requests to produce an export beer. They received mixed replies. In December 1885 William Maile wrote to Henry Parker of Bondi, in Sydney, Australia '...we do not brew ales for exportation and fear if forwarded these would do us no credit nor give satisfaction to you...as our ale and beer is brewed from malt and hops only they are delicate and are much more likely to feel change of temperature...but thank you again for your enquiry...'[262]

A similar request came from L Peake at Malang in Sarawak in April 1885. The reply stated '...we have made enquiry of the shippers but find no steamers for some weeks to ship our ales...we fear if they are forwarded now in such hot weather it would do us no credit nor give satisfaction to you...we regret the order was not received earlier...' By December 1887 beer was going to Sarawak, although...'the troopship is refusing goods so we must find another route...[263]' In April 1890 payment of the account was being chased.

A modest arrangement was made with Crofts, the London port company, to export some products to Oporto. In May 1887 Mr Maile wrote to the Camberwell Stores asking for sailing times. In July he wrote to R H Power in Oporto thanking him for the safe return of the casks and saying '...we prefer not to export summer brewed beers ...wait until October... this could well lead to business...'[264] This never materialised as in May 1888 Percy wrote to Sir John Croft '...I am much disappointed at the report...the beer was sent when it was very cold and snowy which may have influenced it...therefore it is not wise to send any more at present...'[265]

Advertising was also sanctioned, or not, by Percy. In December 1890 he wrote '...I was much surprised to see an advertisement in The Whitstable Echo without my sanction...'[266] In August 1886 he wrote that '... we don't want to advertise further in the Ramsgate district at present...'

Percy relied upon the professional services of a limited number of people, but especially Benjamin Adkins, the Faversham surveyor and architect. Not only did he design and oversee the construction all the new brewery buildings from 1864 to the 1890s but oversaw all the repairs to brewery houses. In June 1886 Percy went to visit the Three Squirrels at Stockbury with Adkins and in August 1886 he was in Ashford and then on to the Bonny Cravat at Woodchurch to examine the roof.[267] In may 1888 Percy wrote to E Carden that Adkins would call this week about the papering.[268] In 1889 he wrote '...please pay the account...it is passed as correct by Mr Adkins...

at Sheerness...' In June 1889 he visited both the Fountain at Sheerness, the Falstaff at Ramsgate and the Scotts Greys at Throwley to inspect the houses. By 1891 Adkins was ill and Percy wrote to Mr Court saying '... he was unable to see if the work were done satisfactorily...'[269] In January 1892 George Webb of Tunstall inspected the damage done to the Fountain at Sittingbourne. By March 1892 Percy wrote '...Mr Adkins is not able to return to business for some time...but I shall endeavour to carry on...after so many years association...'[270] In September Percy wrote again '... but I cannot promise our work to anyone that would take his business...' There was a mutual loyalty.[271]

James Tassell, the grandson-in-law of James Shepherd, continued as the solicitor of The Brewery. In May 1887 Percy wrote '..I have spoken to Tassell and the conveyance will be ready in 10 days...'[272] The Brewery bankers were Rigden and Hilton of Market Place, Faversham. Percy signed all the outgoing cheques and wrote personally many of the covering letters.

Percy was the active overseer of the repair and replacement of equipment; brewery fittings, railway trucks and traction engines.

Ongoing and routine replacement of brewery equipment was always necessary following the big refit of the 1860s. In December 1886 he wrote to Carty, brewery engineers, agreeing specifications for work.[273] In April 1887 Carty were at work in The Brewery '...getting on satisfactorily...with the Boiling Back, the Liquor Back and the Mash Tun...but be here early on Tuesday as we are anxious to get it finished...'[274] Later in the month William Maile wrote that due to alterations in the brewing plant they were short of yeast. In 1895 Carty did further work; new wort receivers in teak were installed and a new Back was fitted which leaked '...as the nails were not properly driven...' according to Percy. In the same year a new refrigerator was received and fitted by Lawrence and Co.[275]

Aveling and Porter, the traction engines engineers, provide two engines of six and nine tons for The Brewery. Percy took direct interest in their maintenance and repairs.

In respect to railway trucks in March 1891 Percy wrote to the Midland Waggon Company requesting '... new wheels and axles for our own beer trucks which we bought of your firm many years ago...'[276] In the following month he wrote saying how exceptionally obliged he was over the trouble they had taken. In December 1892 Percy visited the inspector at the Longhedge Works in Wandsworth Road concerning the repair of two wagons. In 1885 there was dispute about the painting of the trucks and Percy wrote '...Mr Ponton of Preston Street has always painted our trucks to our satisfaction...'[277]

Cooperage was another area of Percy's interest. In December 1892 he wrote to Messrs Haldane and Co. '...I will order 100 intermediate pins at 5/3 as a trial...however we prefer to number, brand and bush our own casks...'[278] Whilst there was a cooperage at The Brewery, barrels were repaired but not made there.

Percy had a sharp eye for undue expenditure. In August 1887 he wrote to The London Chatham Dover Railway Company '...looking at the account of Messrs Thomas Wild, they include 2/- per pocket for the carriage of hops...as you always charge 1/6 please credit us with 6d per pocket on the next account...there were two consignments of 120 and 189 pockets...'[279] In March 1888 he wrote to a horse dealer that '...the dray horse is still unfit for work...I enclose £105 on the understanding I return him if not suitable...'[280] Later in the year he wrote to a Mr Chambers that the arrangement was cash on delivery and that he must keep to that arrangement. In June 1890 he wrote that it was the system of The Brewery to be paid on delivery and not by monthly account.

Whilst Percy paid great attention to detail in every aspect of the running of his brewery, he showed little engagement with the wider brewing industry. Only in 1884 did he become a member of The Country Brewers Society, at a cost of 10 guineas per annum.[281] He was required to subscribe £100 for the Guarantee Fund 'for the protection of the trade in the forthcoming Parliament'. In this respect he was like his predecessor Henry Shepherd sen., who was a member for three years, from 1822, but resigned due to their ineffectualness. Rigden had taken a similarly jaundiced view of this trade association. William resigned in 1841 and his sons did not rejoin until 1871. Other Kent brewers, like Cobb of Margate, Leney of Dover, Mackeson of Hythe, Tomson and Wotton of Ramsgate, Styles of Maidstone, Flint of Canterbury and Kidd of Dartford were all members in or by the late 1860s.[282]

Likewise local and national politics had little attraction for Percy, unless they had a direct bearing on his business. In April 1892 he stated in one letter '...it is un-necessary to form a trade committee in the Faversham Division as our present member Mr Knatchbull-Hugessen is very popular and it is my intention to support him...'[283] This MP was a Conservative. In March 1893 Percy wrote to him '...enclosing another batch of petitions against The Liquor Traffic Local Control Bill to present to The House...'[284]

Percy agreed all charitable donations and subscriptions. His guiding principle was set out in a letter of April 1893 '...I will not be a subscriber as we have no property in the Parish...'[285] He did make many small contributions to many local organisations. For example in July 1889 he gave £10 to the Margate Regatta. In 1892 he gave £2.2.0 for the restoration of Bethersden Church. He agreed Christmas donations to station masters and their staff.[286] In May 1886 he made donations to The Smeeth Sick Benefit Society, The Ashford Cottage Gardeners Society, The Sittingbourne National School and Buildings Improvement Fund and The Bethersden Cricket Club.[287] In 1887 he sent £2.2.0 to Lloyds paper Mills at Sittingbourne towards their annual holiday.[288] In March 1888 he sent to Stalisfield's Cricket Club and Clothing Clubs £1 and 10/- with the comment '... Mr Wheler and Mr Rigden are large owners of property in your area...'[289] In February 1893 Percy sent a cheque to The Eastbridge Hospital in Canterbury.[290] His charity was focused.

As Percy was an elector of the governors of organisations like The Sick Boys Home and The Clergy Orphan Corporation he was probably a benefactor there too. In April 1886 he was an honorary member of The Woodchurch Provident Society.[291]

With all these demands on his time Percy appears as a typically hardworking family businessman. If necessary he worked as long as it took to complete urgent business. In February 1893 Mr Bones of the Prince of Wales, Sittingbourne, was expected '...to call without fail at The Brewery at 3 30pm on Saturday...'[292] On New Year's Eve 1887 Percy required a tenant to attend him at The Brewery at 5pm on a Saturday.

The workload of Percy fluctuated as the experience and numbers of staff fluctuated. With the death of William Maile in 1885 he lost a reliable and hard working traveller and general manager, who, after 25 years service, was difficult to replace. Whilst Percy's nephew, Charles Graham, had joined the firm in the early 1880s and his son Harry Sidney Neame was in place by the late 1880s, they had yet to gain the experience of Maile.

Once again it is difficult to establish how Percy spent his free time during these years. Saturday was a working day and Sunday was for '...regular attendance at the Faversham Parish Church...' not Ospringe Church.[293] From the tangential evidence of the Letter Books it was limited. Family life was certainly very significant. 5 more children were born after 1875; Bernard in 1876, who died the following year, Evelyn in 1877, Madeline in 1879, Violet in 1880 and Leslie Guy, the last and youngest, in 1882. In the mid 1880s, with 8 or 9 children from the ages of 20 to 1 at home at The Mount, life must have been hectic, albeit that there was an indoor domestic staff of 5.

The three eldest sons were sent to school, first at Albion House, Cliftonville, Margate, and then to Harrow. Alick played for the Harrow Cricket XI. Where the daughters were educated is as yet unknown.

As Percy's young family was growing up so his old family was dying. His oldest brother Richard Beale Neame, who had retired from farming the family farm of Homestall to live in Hastings, died in 1893 leaving 6 children. His legacy of £5,000 showed how unprofitable farming had become. The next brother Austen Beale Neame died, unmarried, in London in 1886 after a very successful life as a wholesale sugar merchant in the City. His legacy was over £40,000. In 1893 their sister, Elizabeth Beale Neame, the widow of John Henry Mares, who had remarried in 1866 Dr Charles Payne Tomkins, died in Surrey. She had enjoyed a comfortable life on the legacy of her first husband and left 4 daughters from the first marriage and 2 sons from the second. Percy must have felt this loss especially, as it was she who had launched him into the Brewery and retained her family trusts as mortgages on interest there ever since.

The summary of Percy's first twenty years as sole proprietor of The Brewery must be twofold; firstly of consolidation of what he had borrowed a great deal of money to purchase and secondly of dedicated attendance to his business. He was a conservative hardworking family man in a saturated sector. Percy was no great innovator but he was committed professionally to making a success of what he had.

CHAPTER FIVE

Percy Neame Handing Over 1895-1913

In 1896 Percy Neame was 60. He was an old man for that generation yet he continued to run his brewery as sole proprietor for another 17 years. During those years there were new initiatives, that may have been promoted by three of his four sons whom he brought into the business. One at least ultimately saved The Brewery from failure. There was no resistance to change once it's potential had been proven but there was no fundamental change that might have put The Brewery at risk. However, despite rising turnover there were declining profits in the later years. What Percy did allow himself much more time for in these years were the traditional country interests outside his business; farming, cricket and fox hunting.

The Brewery balance sheet of these years continued to grow, but not at the rate of the previous 20 years. In 1895 the net assets or 'Capital Balance' stood at £135,000. By 1912 they had grown to £173,000. That is by 27% or less than 2% per annum; very different from the annual rate of growth of over 5% in the previous 17 years.[294]

Despite a stagnant market Percy produced increases in the sales turnover of The Brewery from the late 1890s. In 1878 turnover stood at £83,000, dropped to £70,000 in 1880 and by 1895 had fallen further to £65,000. Thereafter there was a sharp up-turn. In 1900 the turnover was £89,000 and despite a few fluctuations in 1912 the turnover was just short of £100,000. A 50% increase in 20 years was a little below 2% per annum; ahead of inflation.

The Profit and Loss Account for these years reflected general market conditions. A steady decline in net profits from 1900 in both absolute terms and expressed as a percentage of turnover and net assets. Each year Percy continued to take 5% of the net assets deemed as 'return on capital he had invested'. In addition as sole proprietor he took the remaining net profit himself. In 1878 net profit was £13,000. In 1880 it had halved and in 1890 had dropped further to £4,600. From 1895 to 1905 there was a recovery and then a collapse. In 1910 the net profit was a mere £783 and in 1912 only £1,400. From the 1880s Percy paid himself in addition a salary of £725 per annum.

Most of these trends can be explained by and followed through the fine range of company books that survive for the period; the Balance Books, the Journals, the General Out Letter Books, the Stock Books, the Malt Books and the Private Ledgers. These were kept by a small office of probably 4 clerks. Many sections of the Private Ledger were written by Percy himself until June 1910, two years before his death.[295] He was a significant letter writer on all subjects concerning his business, but especially the public houses and product quality, until virtually the end.

Mortgages and loans continued to be an important part of the balance sheet. Between 1895 and 1913 they grew steeply from £60,000 to £105,000. The debt holders continued to be family members plus long standing local friends. By 1901 of the mortgages of £101,000 the immediate Neame family, including some of the children of Percy, held £55,000; the Graham cousins held £7,500; the Mares nieces held £9,000; William Maile's daughter, Mrs Cobb of Throwley, held £1,500; the Tassells held £20,000; and the remainder of £8,000 was held by Smith's Bank and a handful of old friends. In other words 70% of the debt was held by the extended Neame family. It was a family business upon whose fortunes the family ultimately relied despite Percy being the sole proprietor. He clearly carried his family with him.

By 1913 the mortgages of £105,000 were still held predominantly by the Neame family but loans from Smiths Bank, previously the local Hilton Rigden Bank of Faversham, had risen to £13,000. The local economy was intermeshed and self dependent.[296]

Investment in all sections of the business was ongoing, despite a national contraction in beer consumption. The constant investment continued to be in the public houses estate, both by new purchases and by incremental improvements. Between 1895 and 1913 6 new houses were added to the portfolio, taking the total number up to 112, still below the high point in 1865 of 129 houses. The number of freeholds increased from 82 to 90 whilst the number of leaseholds fell to 22.

The purchases were spread. In Faversham the Alma at Ospringe was added in 1908 which compensated for the sale of the depressed Masons Arms in West Street to the Faversham Gas Company. At Selling the Old Century was purchased in 1908 and the White Lion leased in 1898. Further afield the Evenhill House at Littlebourne was purchased in 1896, the Crown at Sarre in 1897, the Mackland Arms at Rainham in 1892, the Watermans Arms and the Hero of the Crimea at Sheerness were purchased in 1897 and 1898. The dash to increase the pub estate, so endemic in the brewing industry in these years, was long over for Shepherd Neame.

Incremental improvements to the public houses took a number of forms. Modernisation was the most obvious. The Railway Hotel in Faversham is a good example. This was leased from the Preston Charities and until the coming of the railway to Faversham was a private house. Adaptation to pub use was initially minimal. The only small addition was of a new stable in 1893.[297] In 1899 the southern end was demolished and rebuilt by Fuller and Son of Faversham to the plans of the local architect E Pover and Son. The works were completed in September 1901.[298] The change in style is obvious to this day. Inside separate and independent bar areas were built. A modern hockey stick shaped bar with substantial shelving behind, to carry the popular new bottled beers and spirits, was constructed and in one bar a series of 'snob screens' was introduced. At the side a new reception hall, office and staircase was built. Upstairs new bedrooms were built but bathrooms and lavatories were shared and minimal.

In the country a good example of improvement is easy to follow at the Dove at Dargate. The original building that Percy bought in 1884 was a timber framed thatched beer house at the rear and to the right of the present building. Firstly the main gabled brick block was built at right angles to the old thatched building, then in 1910 the old building was demolished and a new room built to the right.[299] Sometime later the extension to the left went up.

The addition of new rooms used mainly as 'club rooms', for meetings or private functions, was a popular modernisation at this time. They are distinctive to this day; a single story long low room attached to the side of an older taller public house. For example in 1900 new rooms were built at the Duke of Cumberland, Whitstable, the Queens Head, Boughton, Beacon Court, Gillingham and the Bonny Cravat, Woodchurch.[300]

The fitting of the standard public house window can also be dated to these years. A glance at any Georgian pub building shows this. On the first floor are the traditional sash windows. On the ground floor these have been replaced by large two or three sections of long plate glass windows, sometimes etched. Smaller openings are above, often with stained glass.. Sometimes a column divides the sections. The Three Tuns in Tanners Street, the old White Horse in West Street or the Bear in Market Place are just three Faversham examples.

Interior re-fitting driven by technology and changing tastes is evident in the construction of bars. These were designed to take pumps or 'beer engines' as they were called which replaced the tradition of serving beer from casks in the cellar. Shepherd Neame's earliest engines were bought in the 1890s. In November 1891 The Brewery ordered two '...four motion mahogany beer engines with 15 feet of piping...' for the Blacksmiths Arms at Sheerness and the Four Horseshoes at Whitstable. They were supplied by Messrs. George Farmiloe & Sons of 34, St John Street, West Smithfield, London. The following month Beer Engine No. 1010 was ordered from their catalogue plus 60 feet of piping and a man to fit it. This was supplied to Capt. H. G. Cotterill at Royal Marine Barracks, Chatham, a commercial customer of The Brewery.[301]

The average expenditure on 'Repairs and Improvements' to public houses increased significantly after 1900. In the previous 20 years the outlay ranged from £1,600 to £2,000 per annum.[302] Thereafter it ranged from £2,500 to £3,000 per annum. Perhaps this part compensated for only a modest opportunity to outlay on acquisitions in these later years or more likely even then Percy was reacting to changing public demands.

One other capital improvement needs to be mentioned. In 1898 the new Ramsgate stores were completed at a cost of £2,193.

Two other modest types of investment occurred in these years. Percy purchased many small pieces of land attached to public houses. Perhaps these were to cater for slightly more relaxed drinking in a garden or for use for pub outside games. At the same time he was purchasing cottages next to his pubs. The outlay was a few hundred pounds per annum.

Percy's biggest single capital outlay was on upgrading The Brewery plant and premises. After 33 years since the last re-fit, large amounts of money were spent on the production capabilities. In 1897 and 1898 the brew house was totally modernised.[303] The contractors were the leading brewery contractors of their day, William Bradford, who had done so much work on the other side of Court Street for the Rigden Brewery. The engineers were Robert Morton and the builders were the local Ospringe firm of R.M. & H. Whiting. The final bill was £9,896. In 1905 a further £158 was spent on new tuns.

A description of the brew house in May 1897 survives in Percy's hand.

The brew house contained the following rooms:

2 mash tuns for mashing malt, 1 underback, 1 wort receiver, 2 coppers for boiling worts, 1 hop back, 1 wort receiver or pumping back, 1 cooler, 3 refrigerators for cooling worts.
3 hot liquor backs for hot liquor.
20 collecting and fermenting vessels, which vessels were contained in 4 rooms.
In addition there were:
5 rooms for storing malt and hops.
9 rooms for storing beer.

Each of these rooms was marked with a reference letter and number, probably for the Excise men or possibly for reference to a plan now lost.[304]

In 1900 16 Court Street was rebuilt to match 17 Court Street and created the suite of reception area and offices as one building that survive today. The cost was £1,291. Outside, the new Chaff House was completed in 1897. The new Bottling Store was completed in 1899 at a cost of £1,600.

The new Bottled Beer Store was built at a cost of £1,231. The builders for each were the local firm of Whiting. The surveyor for the store was William Bradford & Co. At the Creek side the stables were rebuilt by Gann & Co., specialists in such work.

In 1905 the purchase of 22 Court Street and the range of Jackmans Cottages in Alfred Place behind, for £675, completed the jigsaw of the Court Street site. In the following year the Spirit Stores were built to the designs of the Faversham architect, Edwin Pover, and constructed by Whitings at a cost of £1,672. In 1912 Fullers made further additions to the Bottling Stores.[305] With the exception to these special expenses the average annual repairs bills for the brewery plant were about £600.

Whilst the decision to invest in the plant was ultimately Percy's, the management of all these projects was by his eldest son, Harry Sidney Neame.[306] In September 1896 Harry wrote to Messrs Morton to send down a man to fix the pumps and the new malt hopper which was sitting on The Brewery wharf. By reply Morton advised him that the new copper would be leaving the copper mills the following day. A new boiler and pressure gages were expected at the same time. In October Whitings, the builder, had sketches but needed the centre of the columns agreed by Mortons. In November two new mash tuns were expected and Whitings had the girders ready.

In February 1897 Harry sent more pressing letters to Mortons. 'We are anxious to start working the new plant next week but are only able if our new steam main is ready...unless we are unable to do so it means another weeks delay... The work is progressing and we hope to use the re-fixed waste tun early next week, as soon as we can trust the new machinery. We are prepared to have our other mash tun removed and our old hot liquor back out. Is Carty ready to fix the new hot liquor back and have Buxton and Thornley all the machinery ready for the same? The girders appear to be some time on order for Whitings to fix...' On March 10 he wrote that '...we hope to move the mash tun and hot liquor back next week if Carty's men come on Wednesday...'

Two weeks later Harry wrote to Bradford, the overall contractor saying that '...we are getting the hop back into place today but the cooler and mains to the refrigerator will take two more weeks... we hope the mash tun will be fixed before then...Mortons must send another copper smith and mate...we hope the mash tun will be re fixed by then...the new hot liquor back is ready for the coil. There is at least a month's work for two gangs...'

Once the brew house was dealt with Harry turned his attention to the cask yard. Tenders went out late in 1897. In January 1898 the tender of Semark and Hudson of Faversham for a new cask washing tank was accepted. The lead contractor was again W Bradford. In March a rotary pump mounted on wheels with a 40ft. delivery hose was tried.

In September 1898 work on the boiler was underway. Harry wrote that '... The Brewery had not received the auto-electric feed purifier...that must be fixed before working the boiler next week...' In March 1899 Harry wrote to E K Mitting at Sydenham '...that your auto-electric boiler purifier has been doing all you claimed it would...but as all the boiler pipes are new we will clean the boiler a second time for a trial...' Ultimate sanctions came still from Percy. In May 1898 he wrote a stiff letter to Bradfords asking them to settle the account of Whitings the builder.

With these investments in the plant Percy must have expected an improvement in production and sales and a return on money spent. The figures available suggest a modest improvement in sales. The Shepherd Neame barrelage, which had reached a nadir in the late 1880s of 32,000, had recovered to 35,500 barrels by 1895 and by 1900 had reached 39,612, the highest output for 20 years.[307] The reason for this fluctuation is uncertain but the experience of Shepherd Neame reflected the national averages. Between 1900 and 1914 national sales of beer declined.[308]

The range of beer sold did not alter but the mix of beers sold changed slightly between 1895 and 1912. Bitter continued to be the most popular beer sold and accounted for about 30% of sales by volume. Mild became more popular at 30% of sales and Pale Ale popularity fell from 22% of sales to 12% of sales. The popularity of porter halved to 4%.[309]

Just as the range of beers produced remained remarkably stable so did prices. In 1890 the four India Pales Ales, Stock, No1, No2 and AK were advertised for 60/-, 48/-, 36/- and 34/- per 36 gallons barrel. Mild sold at 36/- per barrel; Table Ale at 28/- per barrel; Table Beer at 24/- per barrel; Stout at 50/-; and Porter at 36/-.[310] Kilderkins, firkins and pins were advertised at correspondingly a half, quarter and eighth of those prices. 17 years later, on 1 January 1907, The Faversham News advertised the same products at the same prices. A discount of 2/- per barrel or 1/- per kilderkin was allowed for cash on delivery.

That the prices remained unaltered over such long periods is not surprising. Consumption of beer per head was static. Population growth was slowed down after the birth rate peaked in 1879. There was no general inflation. There was the ever present competition from Rigden's Brewery in Court Street, opposite the Shepherd Neame Brewery. Here was a very reputable brewer to whom locals could substitute instantly if quality or price faltered. Moreover the cost of the raw ingredient of barley remained static for Shepherd Neame, as home prices were kept down by the impact of foreign imports from North America. The prices of hops fell for much of this period and only started to recover just before The Great War.

Shepherd Neame continued to use Kent hops and local barley only, and always advertised the fact. In 1900 the hops in stock came from only four growers; W & C French, E J Pout, T Powell and Percy's nephews at Homestall Farm Faversham, P & A Neame. The valuations were £4.10.0

per cwt. for the 1899 hops but £6.10.0 for the new Neame hops. In 1905 the average valuation of hop stocks was £9.10.0 per cwt. In January 1913 the stock of fresh 1912 hops was 720 cwt. Those of Lewis Finn, who became Percy's son-in-law, of Westwood Farm and Queen Court Ospringe accounted for 40%. Those of Frederick Neame of Selling, Percy's cousin, accounted for 30%. Stuart Neame, another cousin of Percy, accounted for 10% of his stock. The best price was £7.3.9 per cwt. for the crop of Stuart Neame. The others were valued at £6.6.0 per cwt.[311] Percy controlled the purchase of hops longer than anything else.

The purchasing of barley was gradually handed over by Percy to Harry Neame. This was a further example of how the eldest son was integrated into senior management and direction of the company. In October 1895 Harry wrote '...I will not take this barley...as it has been so cut about by the threshing machine...'[312] In October 1896 he set out the views of The Brewery when he wrote that they were always willing to buy barley direct from growers and had done so especially from Faversham farmers. If growers preferred to deal with them through factors that made no difference.[313] Harry became as diligent as his father in selecting only the best barley. However, Percy would always step in if necessary. In December 1899 he wrote to Mr A J Curling '...I depend upon you to pay your accounts...I shall take the barley and deduct what you owe us...otherwise I shall decline to have anything to do with it...'

The barley came from similar sources to previous years and The Brewery still produced most of its own malt at their three Faversham malt houses. Harry was not averse to looking at other samples. In May 1900 he requested Randells & Co to send samples of Californian malt that The Brewery was considering buying. By November Percy confirmed an order. At the same time Harry bought a very small amount of Indian barley.

The purchase of coal was another area of supply that Harry gradually took over. In July 1901 he agreed to accept a sample of 6-9 tons of coal and some anthracite malting coal from The Great Mountains Collieries Co. However, he warned them that any vessel they chartered to deliver to Faversham '... must not exceed 11ft 6ins. draught...or it will not be able to get up the Faversham Creek...'[314] One problem ensued. On 15 April 1902 Harry discovered arsenic in The Brewery malt despite having been assured that the coal was free from all trace.[315]

The hierarchy of The Brewery's distribution and sales points continued to the end of Percy's life. The largest stores were the Home Stores at The Brewery. In 1907[316] dependent stores were maintained at Canterbury, Herne Bay, Margate, Ramsgate, Sheerness and Sittingbourne. Most were next to the railway stations. Further out stores were at Camberwell, New Brompton, and Penge. Agents were at Birchington, Bridge, Bromley, Dover, Farningham, Folkestone, Lenham, Tenterden, Westgate, Whitstable and Wye. Many of the Agents were wine merchants conducting a modest trade in beer as a sideline. The relative importance of these was unchanged from the previous decades. The vast majority of trade was from the Home Store. From these stores the public houses, private clients and then the clubs were supplied.

Clubs as a source of sales was a new initiative and investment in the last decades of Percy's life. Often housed in impressive new purpose built independent premises they had bars, private rooms and meeting rooms for hire. These clubs were very different from the little ephemeral clubs that met occasionally in 'the club room' of local pubs, like the Faversham Chrysanthemum Club which met at the King William in St Mary's Road, Faversham. They were run by elected committees and had paid servants headed by a steward who was often resident. They produced annual balance sheets.[317] The larger ones were supported financially by The Brewery. Loans were given on mortgage to build, refurbish and equip viable clubs. As the opportunity to purchase pubs was largely over here was a fresh revenue stream and one that could be tied in to The Brewery by loans, service contracts and exclusivity agreements.[318]

The earliest known Brewery trade with clubs was about 1890.[319] They were of various types. There were 'gentleman's clubs', social clubs, political clubs, services clubs, women's clubs, sports clubs and especially working men's clubs. In Faversham The Brewery supplied the Faversham Club, the Artillery Club and the Golf Club from at least 1906. Further out they supplied the Swanley Junction Working Men's Club, possibly from 1889, and certainly from 1905, the Victoria Working Men's Club in Sheerness, founded in 1874, from at least 1904, and the Tilbury Dock Working Men's Club from about 1913. The Sydenham and Forest Hill Liberal and Radical Club was supplied from 1905, the West Norwood Reform Club was supplied from at least 1906 and the Hatcham Liberal Club was supplied from 1910.

Regular contact was maintained with the clubs by the travellers of The Brewery. Percy Ellis and Douglas Cornfoot were diligent brewery employees as their letters show.[320] Later were Sidney Brown and Mr Pepper. They reported to George Boorman who reported to Percy Neame.

The additional trade these institutions generated was very substantial. By 1911 The Brewery supplied 30 clubs; by 1921 they supplied 90 clubs and by 1931 they supplied 184 clubs. In 1921 60% of the production of The Brewery was sold to clubs. As more beer was consumed per head in clubs than in public houses it is probable that in 1911, when The Brewery had 112 public houses and 30 clubs, that 20% of the Brewery trade was to clubs.[321] It is conceivable that this new income stream saved The Brewery from closure or a takeover.

At the same time as clubs were developed as a new sales outlet for The Brewery, a new way of delivering beer was embraced. The sale of beer in bottles, rather than exclusively in barrels or tuns, became popular. They were easy to handle and the investment was relatively cheap.

The Brewery had been experimenting with bottled beer and bottling from about 1887 but in a limited way. Cautious testing of the market place before making a big financial commitment was usual practice at The Brewery. The initiative to bottle beer appears to have come to Percy from Croft the port merchants offering trade outlets in the Far East.

The first reference to Shepherd Neame bottled beer is in a letter from Percy to John Croft[322] in July 1887 in which he says '...it is impossible to bottle any more until October...' In October William Maile refers to Pale Ale No 2 being bottled in screw top imperial pints for despatch to Sarawak. In December 1887 William Maile ordered 6 gross of bottles, 1 1/2 gross of screw tops and 2 gross of ale bottles; a total of nearly 1,400 bottles. In May 1888 Maile quoted that it was quite late enough to bottle beers in England now. All was not quite well for in August 1888 Percy wrote to John Croft '...I am obliged for the analysis of the beer in Mr Hobson's report...no more can be done in that respect...we could dispose of the ales we have bottled elsewhere...probably in India...'[323]

By August 1892 The Brewery's bottled beer trade was developing locally, but not yet to public houses. Mr Charles Holmes the Faversham grocer at 1 Court Street bought 1 gross of bottles of ale at 2/- per dozen.[324]

Nor did The Brewery have its own bottling plant this early. The bottling was done by wine merchants; H Minter at Westgate, Shaxby Bros. at Canterbury and Ashford and R J Passby at Chatham.[325] In 1892 The Brewery used plain bottles to which it attached its own printed labels. By 1896 The Brewery clearly had a trade in bottled beer. A letter to the Park Tavern at Sittingbourne dated 5 May From George Boorman stated '...I have spoken to Mr Neame but he does not feel disposed to put in the Bottle and Jug entrance at present...'[326]

The exact date of bringing the bottling process in house is unclear but in March 1899 Percy wrote to Mr Shaxby '...it is not our intention to bottle any beer before October next...when we shall take the whole of the supply of ales and stouts in bottles of all our houses...' In another letter a few days later this was re-iterated with the comment that '...all our tenants will be supplied direct from here...'[327] Despite this announcement in 1904 Messrs T W Denny, wine merchants at Westgate, were to be supplied by Caustons with 5,000 light summer ale labels, presumably because they did some bottling or processing.[328] By 1909 The Brewery had a 'siphon filling machine' supplied from a firm in Minories, London, and was looking at a labelling machine.[329] This new department was gradually taken over by Arthur Neame, the second of Percy's sons.

In 1912 one foresighted initiative was made to extend both the range of bottled beer and the use of the plant. Harry Neame sent a letter to six breweries in Brussels and Louvain concerning their lagers. One of the recipients was Brasserie Artois. He wrote '...We are desirous of importing a light larger beer for bottling on our premises and supplying the wholesale trade. Your brewings have been recommended to us and we shall deem it a favour if you will send us samples at the same time quoting your lowest terms per hectolitre, from Ostend...'[330] The replies are not recorded but any negotiation would have been cut short by the Great War, two years later.

The popularity of bottled beers, at least in the pubs, was sluggish. By 1908 the public houses were taking large numbers of crates of bottled beer.[331] Beacon Court at New Brompton took 1272 crates of a dozen bottles; the Victoria at Ashford took 758; the Fountain at Sittingbourne took 586; the Duke of Cumberland at Whitstable took 557; and the Railway Hotel at Faversham took 546 crates of a dozen bottles. However, the volumes were small when 1 crate, containing 12 pint bottles, was translated into barrels.[323] For example Beacon Court took 898 barrels of beer but the equivalent of only 53 barrels of beer in pint bottles. In Faversham the Railway Hotel took 278 barrels of beer and the equivalent of 24 barrels of beer in bottles; and St Anne's Cross took 594 barrels of beer and the equivalent of only 19 barrels of beer in bottles. The Brewery did not send bottled beers to London at this date. The costs of producing bottled beer must have resulted in prices that were not sufficiently competitive for the public houses at that date.[333]

Despite this initiative no record survives of what contribution bottled beer made to the Profit and Loss Account. It was probably small if the volumes sold through the public houses are a guide.

At the same time as the initiatives of sales through clubs and producing bottled beers were introduced, the third initiative in the late nineteenth century of The Brewery was the development of a wine and spirits trade. It is not difficult to understand why. The sales of beer appeared to have peaked; other breweries were doing the same as it complemented their core trade; and as Percy had three sons to integrate into the business it was a good way to give them a little commercial independence and training in management. The most pressing reason was probably because the competing brewery in Faversham, Rigden's over the road, was doing the same.

The business plan was to sell to both the tied trade and to the general public. The competition for the latter in Faversham was modest. Dan's was past its peak. Valentine Court at 75 Preston Street, still called The Old Wine Vaults today, was modest. Charles Holmes at 1 Court Street were primarily grocers, albeit ones who prided themselves as 'Agents for Messrs Gilbey, Wine and Spirit Merchants, London'.

In 1896 Alick Percy Neame, a younger 24 years old son of Percy, established this new department at The Brewery. The stock was modest but must have reflected drinking habits of the area of the day. In the earliest 1897 Price List spirits and cordials predominate. The spirits offered were 1 cognac, 1 rum, 3 gins, 6 brandies and 8 whiskeys. Seven cordials were offered of 3 cherry brandies, 1 ginger brandy, and the now forgotten cloves, shrub, peppermint, spruce and sloe gin. In the wine list was 1 sherry, 3 ports and 2 clarets. In total 34 products were offered.[334]

The stock range expanded quickly. By 1910 9 rums, 9 cognacs, 8 brandies, 17 ports, 7 sherries, and 28 whiskeys were on offer. Taste for wine had developed as 8 burgundies, 15 clarets, 13 champagnes, 13 hocks and moselles, 1 Australian, 1 Spanish and British wines such as cowslip and wincarnis were on offer. In addition 16 liqueurs and 2 vermouths were on offer.[335]

Most of the spirits arrived at The Brewery in casks and a little came ready bottled. The Brewery had at least 15 vats containing 350 gallons each of whisky, rum and gin. Smaller amounts of port, cherry brandy and ginger brandy were also kept in vats. Most orders were made up by hand and whiskies were bottled under their own labels. Spirit jars, 1 gallon jars and labels came from London. Most wine came ready bottled.[336]

Transport of spirits to Faversham was by sea and railway. In 1897 Corbett Brown & Co. wrote from Belfast '...we will forward your order by tomorrow's steamer to Dover...' In the same year R. Thorne & Sons wrote '...we will deliver whiskeys free to you at Faversham and we will pay the carriage on empties back to Scotland, provided you send them by rail to Dover thence by Clyde Shipping Co. to us...' Wines came to Faversham from London by rail.[337]

This new department meant new personnel. At first the authority of Alick Neame was limited to negotiating prices but not selecting the stock. He reported to Mr Boorman who reported to Percy Neame. None of them had any professional knowledge of the wine and spirit trade. Gradually Alick acquired discretion over buying. Under him was the head clerk, who from 1899 until his retirement 50 years later, was Harry Jarman Balls. below him were a couple of clerks and a few men in the store who made up orders. The distribution was integrated into the main brewery network of stores, agencies and delivery drays.

The reaction of most public house tenants to these new opportunities is not recorded but a few amusing letters survive. Mr Bisley, an agent at The Plough and Harrow at Bridge, wrote '...I could with your assistance do something in the bottle trade but I cannot afford to speculate on stock...I need a special price list...with a special heading...' Three weeks later he wrote again '...the Irish Whiskey you sent is poor quality...it has done no good for the house...as we have no Scotch Whiskey please send some...Sharp.'[338] In July 1903 Percy Neame wrote a customarily succinct letter to a tenant, Harry Farley, who annoyed him. '...you are perfectly aware that we send spirits to Ashford every Wednesday...we received your order on Thursday...your letter is a great presumption in telling me how to manage my houses...'[339]

Once the department became established new premises were purchased and built for the stores. 19 Court Street was bought and the first stores were built over part of its garden. In 1905 the

the fruit to be picked. In December he noted that the ewes were not doing so well. In February 1896 he gave instructions for 20 sheep to be sent to Canterbury Market and complained soon after that they had been over driven as some arrived lame. At the same time he asked when the cow would calf. In November he was concerned that Mr Fittall's ram did not get with the ewes as they were old and had bad teeth.

In August 1897 he was asking for 8 couples of his ducks to be sent to him. In October 1899 Percy did not want too many hurdles and asked for cake and oats for the sheep and not barley. In March 1903 Percy was instructing Mr Newport to turn the mare out at Forresters Lodge but that it was useless to turn out the colt at Stone Street. He wanted the colt broken and fed with corn.

Percy was a regular visitor to his farms on Saturday afternoons which stretched to Fridays in his later years. He usually travelled to Canterbury by train and was met by a hansom cab or a carriage to take him on when he went to the Stone Street farm. He probably used his own carriage to get to Forresters Lodge, which was only 4 miles from home.

Cricket was a lifetime interest of Percy. 'In his younger days he was a player of considerable ability and even when he was well over 50 he still enjoyed the game. He maintained an excellent ground at The Mount, where for many years the old Faversham Club used to play. From 1892 to 1912 an annual match was played there on Whit Monday on behalf of the funds of the Faversham Cottage Hospital and the Dispensary. On these occasions he used to entertain the teams to lunch most hospitably but in the last few years his genial presence at the head of the table has been much regretted'.[354] His son Alick Neame especially enjoyed cricket and brought his Cambridge friends home to play. Local newspapers reported in full each year the results of all these Saturday afternoon matches.

Percy was also a member of the Kent County Cricket Club. He was a member of the General Committee from 1898 to 1901, when he was 65. From at least 1902 to 1912 he took a tent at the Canterbury Cricket Week. The tents adjoining his, No 15 or No 16, were those of either Sir Edwyn Dawes of Mount Ephraim, Hernhill, or The Old Stagers, and the Mayor of Canterbury.[355]

Percy's third great interest was fox hunting, at the centre of rural life and then the biggest spectator sport in England. The huge crowds seen at meets far outnumbered those at football matches. He was a great supporter of and rode with The Tickham Hunt, whose master was his brewing competitor in Court Street Mr Rigden. The Easter Monday and Boxing Day meets met regularly at the Mount and were entertained by him. He was also Chairman of the Farmers Committee of the Hunt. This passion was inherited by his daughter Madeleine.

Relaxation for Percy and his family during the summer extended to the regular leasing of a house at Westgate, next to Margate. Here was a smart new development, cut off from the increasingly popularised Margate. It had grown gradually from the 1870s and had something originally of the feel of Le Touquet on the Kent coast. Percy's wife, Madame, moved there in the spring until the autumn but Percy spent only the occasional week here. In April 1909 instructions were sent to Mr Maybourne, The Brewery store man at Margate, that '...the furniture wines, spirits and 2 kilderkins of AKK were to be moved next Saturday for Mr Neame to Somerville House, Westgate Bay and the key may be had of Messrs Rogers and Temple Offices near the station...'[356] Here Madame enjoyed entertaining young army officers, one of whom, Clement Cotterill, married her daughter, Ida Neame.[357]

At the same time all Percy's remaining old relations, so important to him in his launch into The Brewery, were dying. His two elder sisters, Fanny Graham and Anne Graham died in 1901 and 1904 and his brother in law Thomas Graham died in 1913. Percy outlived all his generation except his brother in law, John Lawrence Graham, who died in 1922 at Broadstairs, aged 93.

Percy's family network however was, and remained, immense by today's standards[358] In his generation he had 6 brothers and sisters and 31 Neame first cousins. In the next generation he had 10 children, 19 Neame nieces and nephews and about 50 Neame second cousins once removed. In the following generation he had 21 grandchildren, 30 Neame great nieces and nephews and countless cousins. With spouses these numbers were increased substantially.

Percy's children were marrying. The sons remained very much tied to Faversham but the girls were leading independent lives.

Harry Sidney, the eldest son, married Maud Cobb from the brewing family at Margate. They lived at Alfred House, London Road, Faversham from the 1890s.[359]

Arthur the second son remained unmarried and lived at home at The Mount until his father died in 1913 and then moved with his brother, Alick, to Shirley on the London Road, Faversham. He joined The Brewery in the 1890s. Before The Great War he was an officer in The Faversham Volunteers but was called up in 1914. He took command of The Kent 2nd Heavy Battery, Royal Garrison Artillery. He was promoted major but died of pneumonia at Ightham, Kent in 1916. He was buried at Ospringe churchyard. His nephew described him as '...a large red haired man...with wet lips and hot hands...'

Alick Percy the third son remained unmarried. He was considered the most intelligent of the entire family.[360] He went up to Trinity Hall Cambridge in 1891 and he graduated BA in 1895.[361] He returned to Faversham and joined The Brewery immediately. His passion was cricket. He was the only member of the family to become a Faversham Town Councillor, for three years from 1913. He was not called up for the Great War. He died in 1916 and is buried with his brother at Ospringe.[362] Neither of these two sons liked their mother, whom they considered disloyal to their father.

Leslie Guy, the youngest of all the children was totally different. He was charming but weak. He was always in need of money and was always staying with his relations, who liked him. Mary Dawes remembered him as a frequent visitor to Lorenden. In 1911 he was described as a student of agriculture[363] but there is no record of him ever having a job. From a number of letters to his brother Harry in the 1920s he always had ideas about new schemes that would make a fortune or requests for money to settle a tailors bill for clothes '...a chap must have...'[364]

There is no record of him serving during The Great War[365] but in summer 1917 he married in Chelsea a French woman, Raymonde Cornillot, whom some in the family thought was a 'lady of ill repute'. They had two children, Serge and Michelle Neame, whom he later disowned. They were divorced in the 1920s but as late as 1956 Raymonde wrote to Jasper Neame, her nephew by marriage, asking for help, saying that Percy used to help her.[366] When Leslie died in 1938 at Worcester Park Surrey he left his mere £755 to a Helen Margaret Tomkins, spinster.[367]

Percy's eldest daughter, Marion, married Alaric Watts Churchward, 21 years her senior.[368] She was described by her nephew as '...Aunt May was tall, deaf but very nice...who gave all her nephews and nieces money regularly...her husband was a very jolly fellow who after some years at Queenborough, Kent became the manager in Paris of the London Chatham and Dover Railway Company...consequently they had some very good French furniture...'

They had one son, Percy Alaric Churchward, who was born in Paris and was employed by the railway company as a clerk at Dover. During the Great War he joined the Royal Transportation Establishment as a Sapper and was killed at the end of the war. He was buried at Blargies Communal Cemetery Extension, Oise in France.[369]

Florence Neame, or Dolly, married Col. Johnson RE. His family were very prosperous jute merchants. They lived at Elgin in Scotland. He was described as '... an enormous man who played the viola and she as very sweet...'

Ida married Clement Morton London Cotterill. His father had made a fortune out of jute in the mid nineteenth century. He settled at Hawkhurst, Kent, where in the 1870s he built a suitably grand house, Tongswood, from the proceeds.(Now St Ronans School). Clement was an army officer, who was an admirer of Madame, but later was described as a stockbroker. He spent the later part of his life in a wheelchair at their house in Bromley but nothing was left of his father's fortune. She was described as '... a very jolly person, who blossomed as a merry widow, drove fast cars and went dancing at Palais de Danse, such as Locarno at Streatham...'

Evelyn married Harold Abbott Barnes. He was a doctor in the Medway.

Madeleine married Lewis Finn, who was brought up at Westwood Farm near Faversham. He later bought and farmed Queen Court Farm, Ospringe. He was a very successful farmer not least because he refused to join The Hop Marketing Board when it started. He lived at Lorenden, Ospringe. Maddie was red haired and rather combatative, according to her nephew. She was Master of the Tickham Hunt.

Violet was described as very sweet indeed. She married James Kerr of Coates Cotton, a very rich man. He was an austere Presbyterian. He held daily prayers before breakfast for the entire household. He refused to use cars on Sundays so everyone had a two miles walk to church and back. He forbade drink in the house except beer for guests at dinner if they ordered it upon arrival. The Kerrs were regular visitors to Lenzerheide. They lived at Invery, Banchory.

The link of all these is not only Percy, their father, The Master, but their mother his wife, Madame. She has been variously described by a grandson, as having admirers and of being fabulous material for a Rogue Herries type novel; and by a granddaughter, as plainly a nymphomaniac.

She was 10 years younger than Percy and by at least 1911 was enjoying the pattern of life she followed after his death for the rest of her life. She was staying at The Grand Mansions, Folkestone, with her admirer Captain Graham and her favourite son Leslie Guy Neame. She doted on both of them.

CHAPTER SIX

Aftermath

Percy died at The Mount on Sunday afternoon on 5 January 1913 aged 76.[370] He was buried three days later in Ospringe Churchyard, not because this was his church but because the churchyard at Faversham where he attended was closed for new burials. He was interred next to his infant son Bernard and his mother-in-law.

The funeral drew 'a very large attendance of townspeople and residents in the neighbourhood.' The mourning coaches were preceded by over 70 Brewery employees, each of whom carried a floral tribute. They were followed by the main family mourners, who, by a rather outdated tradition, excluded all women. They were followed by the indoor servants, the office staff and then local residents, all of whom were male. It was a roll call of local families, but not a single Shepherd was listed; Lord Harris, Hon. Henry Milles-Lade, Neames, Hiltons, Barnes, Dawes, Vallance, Stunt, Finn, Gillett, Millen, Minter, Tett and the Chief Ticket Collector of the LCD Railway Company, Mr Spillett. The tenants of the houses waited inside the church.

Percy's will summarised his wishes for the future. The execution of it quantified the true state of his assets and his achievements and the reality of inheritance. Percy's estate consisted almost entirely of the assets of The Brewery. His other assets were minimal.

His will was drawn up in 1904 and modified in 1911. His trustees and executors were his eldest sons, Harry and Arthur and his nephew Charles Graham. It was a simple will. He confirmed to each of his three eldest sons £10,000 already given them; to each of his daughters £2,500 plus whatever he had given them; to Florence his wife an annuity of £3,500 pa for life; to all his children equally the residual estate. He provided for the continuation of his brewery by offering it to his three eldest sons, Harry, Arthur and Alick, at a price to be agreed by valuers and which would be paid into his residual estate. It was pragmatic, fair and not restrictive. It was very similar to the wills of Julius and Henry Shepherd a century before; transfer of a lifetimes hard work to all the children, with a proviso that those in the next generation who had committed to the future of the business should have the first option to buy out their siblings.

After the funeral the three sons considered the possibilities of purchasing the business, which they wished to do, but they decided that they had no means to do so. This was ostensibly because of the liabilities of Percy, for which his other property was insufficient to provide. It was probably because they were terrified at the challenge of taking on a huge mortgage; unlike their father 60 years previously or Henry Shepherd jun. in 1844.

The family were then faced with how to raise sufficient money to pay the legacies under the will. Three options were considered: retain the business in the family but capitalise it as a limited company; sell the business as a going concern; or break it up and sell the parts.[371] They had to begin by valuing The Brewery assets for the options facing them.

Valuation for the first option consisted of: loans on mortgage of £19,000, loose plant and stock of £23,000, licenses and goodwill if any of £1,000 and the major asset of freehold and leasehold property and fixed plant of £189,000. The total was £232,000. The book debts of £28,000 due to Percy were retained by the trustees.

Valuation for the second option was not completed. The auditor stated 'From my extensive knowledge of Brewery companies and the present state of the market of shares in such companies it would be impracticable to get the necessary capital subscribed by the public in cash at the present time (of consolidation). I am also firmly of the opinion, and I have advised the executors, that it would be impracticable to find a purchaser at a price which would discharge all the liabilities for which the testators private estate would be insufficient to provide the legacies... especially the widow's annuity'.

Valuation for the third option was likewise not completed. The auditor stated 'The aggregate sum to be realised by breaking up such a business is highly speculative and the process of realisation would take a considerable time to complete. The brewery and site are entirely unsuited for use as any other class of business and would be practically un-saleable without the licensed houses. The malting premises although more readily realisable are old fashioned and might remain unsold for a long period. The licensed and unlicensed properties could be readily sold. The sale of chattels in use as a going concern would produce a heavy loss. The sale of the book debts and consumable stock would probably realise the amount at which they stand in the testators books. I estimate that such a sale piecemeal would realise sufficient to pay the pecuniary legacies and testamentary expenses but may be insufficient to invest to produce the widow's annuity'.

Further comments were made to the trustees by Mr Mason the auditor to explain the state of the business in Percy's later years which give a contemporary insight into The Brewery at his death.

'He took a keen interest in the affairs of The Brewery and for about 45 years gave it his constant and continuous attention. Although during the last three years of his life he was incapacitated from taking the active part in the management of The Brewery he had, his three sons nominally carried on the business but he did not cease up to the time of his death to require them to consult him on the working from day to day. His sons carried on the business under his direction for 25, 23 and 18 years respectively and they are wholly and his daughters largely dependent upon the business for their income. As they have spent their entire lives in the business they are unfitted for any other calling and it is extremely doubtful whether they would be able to obtain occupation in other breweries owing to the tendency to amalgamation which exists at present.'

Mr Mason went on to talk about the probability of increased profit under younger management. 'Mr Neame's remarkably conservative disposition and the unusual latitude he extended to his customers have mitigated against the progress of the business. I consider the business is capable of showing better results and the current accounts do show that under the improved management of the three sons. I consider that the return on capital could be about 6 1/3%'.

Mr Mason advised the trustees to retain the business in the family, the children concurred and they asked the trustees to draft a scheme for forming a company to purchase the assets of the business. The scheme was agreed, in accordance with the first valuation, and the shares and debentures in the company were then accepted by each of the family in settlement of their legacies. The Memorandum of Agreement was drafted by 22 June 1914[372] and the new company of Shepherd Neame Ltd. was registered on 11 November 1914.

The new company was capitalised by 100,000 5% preference shares of £1 each; 70,000 ordinary shares of £1 each ; and 166 debentures of £100 each, bearing 4% interest, with the option to issue a further debenture of £36,000 maximum, bearing 5% interest. The shares were allocated to achieve the terms of Percy's will.

The preference shares were allocated first: the trustees were allocated 70,000 from which to pay the £3,500 annuity to Percy's widow, Florence, for her lifetime; Harry was allocated 4,100; Arthur was allocated 4000; Alick was allocated 3,800; Leslie was allocated 2,500 and Charles Graham was allocated 600; the remainder were allocated to the trustees.

The ordinary shares were allocated next: Harry was allocated 8,614; Arthur was allocated 6,371; Alick was allocated 5,972; Leslie was allocated 5,233; and the 6 daughters were allocated 2,500 each. A further allocation of 10,000 ordinary shares was made for cash to each of the 10 children.

The debentures were issued last in varying amounts. Percy's widow received 40, Mrs Churchward 36, Miss F Louise Neame 25, and other sons and daughters received descending amounts.

The first Board Meeting was held at The Brewery on 16 November 1914.[373] Harry Neame was elected Managing Director, Arthur and Alick Neame were elected directors. George Ernest Boorman was appointed Company Secretary (the first). Guy Tassell, who was in attendance, was appointed solicitor and Mason & Son were appointed accountants and auditors. All cheques were to be filled by Henry Wilkinson. Other routine business followed. It was finally agreed that a weekly board meeting be held on Thursday. The transfer from sole proprietor company to limited company was complete.

Percy's widow, Madame, really did become the merry widow. Her income was secured for life whatever the performance of the business. Her £3,500 was approximately 25 % of the anticipated annual profit. It is interesting that in 1904 Percy left her an income of less than half that and in 1911 he left her so much more. That final will was witnessed by Dr Gowland,[374] the family doctor, and Mr Tassell, the family solicitor. Perhaps even at that late stage she still charmed them all.

Madame left The Mount immediately and moved to Weybridge, Surrey. Two years later in 1915 she re-married, Major Charles Oliver Frederick Graham, possibly a cousin of Percy's Graham brothers-in-law, in Paddington. She was 66 and he was 36. It is not surprising that the family is supposed to have loathed him.[375]

Charles Graham was, however, no mere pimp, albeit that in his photograph he looks 'jaunty'. He led a far from worthless life.[376] In 1896 he joined the Royal Marines Light Infantry and by 1902 was promoted captain. He served in N Nigeria where he was mentioned in despatches and where his conduct, professional, knowledge and temperate habits were noted as very good. He was described as a very zealous young officer with good judgement and good physical qualities. From 1899 to 1906 he was with the West Africa Frontier Forces, serving in Gambia. From 1907 to 1910 he was attached to the Chatham Division. In 1910 he retired with a gratuity of £1,200 but was appointed to the R M Reserve of Officers.

On 1 August 1914 he was recalled to service as war broke out. On 30 September 1914 he was posted to Belgium in the Royal Navy Air Service. In April 1915 he was with the Chatham Battalion of the Royal Marines at Port Said and landed at Gallipoli. He was wounded at Anzac and invalided to England in July. Here he was promoted major and Camp Commandant at Bedenham. In 1919 he was invested with the Order of the British Empire for his work during the War. He was relegated to the Reserve of Officers, was recalled for service during the 1921 Coal Strike emergency and was finally removed from the reserve of officers in 1927 aged 50.

On leaving the service he took up his special interest, the care of ex servicemen and their families. He became the Hon. Sec. of the Soldiers, Sailors and Airmen's Families Association and then District Head of the Soldiers and Sailors Help Society. From 1922 to 1931 he served on Gosport Borough Council. After 3 years break he returned and then became a County Councillor. 'He had a reputation for getting things done and encouraging everyone to pull their weight'. In 1937 he organised a splendid Coronation Ball at Gosport. He was also a prominent Freemason and Past Master.[377]

Florence and Charles Graham lived at Alverstoke in Hampshire. In the last year of her life she moved to The Queens Hotel, Southsea, where she died in 1934. In the following year Charles remarried another widow, Charlotte Lunaft. He was 59 and she was 80. Charles died at Alverstoke in 1940 aged 63 and his second widow died at Alverstoke ten years later aged 94. Florence left her entire estate of £3,500 to her feckless youngest son Leslie Guy Neame.

For her family Madame as a widow was remote. Mary Dawes believed that her grandmother never returned to Faversham after remarriage. She was certainly not buried with Percy. Her abiding memory of her grandmother was of her annual trip to London Zoo and taking all her grandchildren for a treat. She was dressed immaculately and was propelled around in a bath chair.

In Faversham Percy's eldest three sons were faced immediately after the recapitalising of the business with the outbreak of war. Demand for their product had fallen as Faversham's old industries of brick making and cement making had closed and unemployment had risen. Trying to modernise a run-down plant with military demand taking all available resources was impossible. Planning for production when the raw ingredients of hops and barley were likely to be rationed was challenging. Replacing young men who enlisted or later were called up was a new phenomenon. Government introduced restrictions on output and quality and increased taxation and price control. Then in 1916 two of Harry Neames brothers Arthur and Alick died.

Uncertainty must have been terrifying at times for both Harry as chairman and for his brothers and sisters whose incomes depended upon him. His dedication and hard work to solve unique problems, unknown to Percy, and to make a profit for his family, must have saved The Brewery. The experience he gained of running the business in war time in turn was passed on to his successor sons, Jasper and Laurence Neame, who faced the same problems in 1939.

Percy was described by his auditor Mr Mason as conservative. That characteristic is probably key to understanding him and summarising his life. Whilst he had a wide and close family he had no father to guide him and with only a few thousand pounds capital of his own he borrowed tens of thousands of pounds from his family to invest in a business he knew initially nothing about. He learned his business by trial and error.

Paying down debt, and towards the end of his life trying to do it in a falling market, and fear of losing his family their fortune, must have made prudence central to his life. As he saw his net assets grow, and if he were by nature cautious, he would not have wished to do anything to compromise that. He was not a great innovator , he was professional, businesslike and committed to his brewery. He was under no corporate pressure to maximise returns; by annual incremental growth these far exceeded the inflation of the day. However inefficient his business was towards the end of his life he was a success.

To die the richest man in Faversham, to leave an estate of £240,00, after a personal original investment of only £3,000, and to leave a business that continues as a family business a century later was no mean feat.

Footnotes

Chapter One

1. Lower Garrington.
2. Neame Pedigree 1. Taken from P.G. Selby. The Faversham Farmers Club. 1927. An amended version in text is on the Neame Website. This was based on research of the late Alan Neame of Selling.
3. Sondes Estate Rent Books. Watson Collection (WR). Rockingham Castle, Northamptonshire. Ref: WR.A 7/12.
4. Selling Churchwardens Accounts. Canterbury Cathedral Archive. (CCA). Ref: U3/229/5/A1.
5. Op. Cit.
6. WR. Ref: WR. 557.
7. Sun Fire Office. Insurance Policy No. 690309. London Metropolitan Archives.
8. Sondes Rentals. Kent History and Library Centre (KHLC) Maidstone. Ref: U.791. E105/1.
9. Comments by George Adams of an old Shropshire farming family.
10. C. Greenwood. Epitome of Kent. 1838.
11. Mitchell and Deane. Abstract of British Historical Statistics. p. 488.
12. Kentish Gazette (KG). 15 June 1802. University of Kent Library (UKC).
13. KG. 11 June 1805. UKC.
14. John Bax was the grandson of Alexander Bax, brewer, and nephew of Mary Bax-Marsh-Shepherd of the Faversham Brewery.
15. KG.7 June 1807. UKC.
16. Morning Herald. 19 June 1800. Burney Newspaper Library. British Library (BL) Digital Newspapers Web Site.
17. P. Selby. Op. Cit.
18. Will. 1817. The National Archive. (TNA). Ref: PROB 11/1596.
19. Land Tax.
20. Will. 1817. TNA. Ref:PROB11.

21. Val Boyd Insley. A Family's History. 2001. The East Kent Levels Minutes, KHLC, Ref: EK/S/M/7, note him as a member of the jury, rather than as a leader of innovation.
22. KG. 23 March 1824.
23. KG. 21 January 1827.
24. KG. 12 May 1834.
25. KG. 20 December 1836.
26. Chislet. Churchwardens Accounts. CCA.
27. As there is also no entry in The Death Duty Registers at TNA this suggests his estate was minimal. His monument survives in Chislet Church.
28. Sondes Rental 1827. WR. Ref: WR A8/4. The Sondes income from their Northamptonshire Estate was about £8,000 pa. and from the Kent Estate about £10,500 pa.
29. KG. 5 March 1822.
30. KG. 2 January and 9 March 1827.
31. KG. 6 May 1834. 1 January and 15 January 1838. Examples only.
32. The Times.13 December 1838. Times Digital Archive. British Library (BL).
33. KG. 29 May 1844 and 25 February 1847. Examples only.
34. The Times. 15 October 1847. BL.
35. KG. 24 May 1826.
36. Corpus Christie College Oxford Archive. Ref: Ha1/69-93.
37. KG. 1828.
38. Dividend Book. 1849. Author's library.
39. KG. 31 March 1836.
40. Selling Parish Books. Ref: U/229. CCA.
41. Parish Tithe Apportionment Lists. Parishes. CCA.
42. KG. 28 May and 20 December 1836.
43. KG. 20 February 1844 and 5 June 1849.
44. KG. 29 October and 18 November 1830.
45. KG. 19 August 1839.
46. KG. 4 March 1845 and 3 February 1846.
47. KG. 10 July 1838.

48. Will. Ref: PROB11/2103. Estate Duty Register. IR27 f.290.
49. Mitchell & Deane . Op. Cit. p.488. Barley and Wheat prices.
50. Selling Parish Churchwardens Accounts. Op Cit.
51. Sondes Rental. Op. Cit. Ref. WR A8/4.
52. Parish Tithes . Op. Cit.
53. Owners of Land. Kent. Published 1873. BL.
54. Selby. Op. Cit.
55. Parish Tithes. Op. Cit.
56. KG. 27 December 1822.
57. KG. 28 May 1836 et al.
58. KG. 14 December 1841.
59. KG. 21 July 1846.
60. Times. 5 December 1854.
61. Times. 13 December 1851.
62. Times. 17 December 1862.
63. Will. Probate Court, Holborn, London.
64. Will. Probate Court.
65. He does not appear on the Neame Pedigree of P. Selby.
66. Selling Parish Churchwardens Accounts. Op Cit.
67. Selling Parish Church. Burial Registers. CCA.
68. Pigot's Directories. 1824, 1832, 1839, 1847. Authors Library.
69. Kent Post Office Directories. 1855, 1859,1862,1866, 1878. Beaney Institute, Canterbury.
70. Neame Web Site.
71. KG.25 March and 1 April 1873. Obituary.
72. Times. 15 December 1852.
73. Times. 15 February and 21 May 1853.
74. A. Bateman. Victorian Canterbury. pp.11, 15 ,40, 41, 79 and 91.
75. KG. 2 March 1824.
76. KG. 31 March 1836. and KFIO Shareholders Register. Authors Library.
77. Times. 10 November 1836.
78. KG. 8 December 1840.
79. Times. 15 August 1845.
80. KG. 12 December 1849.
81. Obituary. Op. Cit.
82. Canterbury Census. 1851. Beaney Institute and Library. Canterbury. A daughter Bertha was born there in 1845. He may have bought it in 1839.
83. PO Directory. 1862 and Census 1871. I have been unable to locate this house today. It was probably near the church but is now demolished and replaced by flats.
84. Will. Probate Court.
85. W. Berry. Pedigrees of Kent. 1830. Beale pedigrees on pp. 19-20, 22-23 and 204.
86. Beale Pedigree 3. Taken from W. Berry pp.22-23. Op. Cit.
87. Will. Pr. 1787. TNA. Ref. PROB 11/1149/172.
88. Will. Pr. 1789. TNA. Ref. PROB 11/1178/331.
89. The site is close to Southwark, the centre of the hop trade. London late C18th maps show the site clearly. In 1872 OS Map of the area lists the name of the wharf with occupiers. In 1914 OS Map it has disappeared and the area has become absorbed in Hays Wharf, the place name that survives today. Map Collections. London Metropolitan Archives, Islington. At least one Faversham merchant, Robert Collier, was using this wharf in the 1780s. See article of J Owen. Two Faversham Merchants. 2001.
90. Will. Pr. 1836. TNA. PCC. Ref. PROB 11/1864/57.

91. See notes on Beale letters by Mrs Pru Stokes below.
92. Biddenden Census. TNA on line.
93. Biddenden Census. TNA on line.
94. Will. Will Register Indexes. Now located at Court 38, The High Court, The Strand, London.
95. See note on Beale Letters below.
96. Tenterden Censuses. TNA on line.
97. J. Owen. The Shepherds and Shepherd Neame Brewery Faversham. 2011.
98. Will. Court 38, High Court, Strand.
99. Maidstone Censuses. TNA. On line.
100. Will. Court 38, High Court, Strand.
101. Various Censuses. TNA. On line.
102. See note on Beale Letters below.
103. Will. Through her and her daughter, Fanny Witherden Pinyon, descended the Beale Letters.
104. Various Censuses. TNA. On line.
105. Various Censuses. TNA. On line.
106. Will. Court 38. High Court, Strand.
107. Various Censuses. TNA. On line.
108. Various Censuses. TNA. On line.

Chapter Two

109. Faversham Tithe Schedules. 1839. CCA. Parish of Faversham.
110. WR. Ref. WR A8/4. Op. Cit.
111. Sondes Estate Rental Summary. 1837. KHLC. Ref. U.1175 E.118. The three Hilton brothers accounted for 11% and the two Cobbs for 7% of the total rental.
112. P. Selby. Op. Cit.
113. KG. 27 December 1822.
114. KG. 2 March 1824.
115. CCA. Freemen Lists.
116. Game Certificate. KG. 7 September 1829.
117. KG. 6 May 1834.
118. KG. 20 December 1836.
119. I am most grateful to Mrs Pru Stokes of Willow Cottage, Biddenden, for the use of her transcripts of the Beale letters and her explanatory notes. The letters cover the years 1809 to 1852 and were written to Mrs Frances Beale (maternal grandmother of Percy Beale Neame) by her children and grandchildren. They were given by her ggg grandson, Rev. Paul Bowen, to the Biddenden Local History Society for the village archives in 1993. 280 letters are arranged in bundles numbered I to XVIII. The majority date from 1848-1852. There are 150 references to and 23 specific letters that concern directly the Neame, Graham and Hilton families.
120. Beale Letters. Bundles I, II & IV. 1809-1818.
121. Beale Letters. Bundle II.
122. Beal Letters. Bundle IV.
123. Beale Letters. Bundle III. There are virtually no more letters until 1848.
124. Death Duty Register. TNA. Ref IR 26/1462 f.581.
125. 1841 Faversham Census. TNA . On line.
126. 1841 and 1851 Faversham Censuses. TNA. On line.
127. Beale Letters. Bundle X/1/D/4.
128. Marriage Certificate 30 September 1844. Faversham Parish Church. TNA.
129. The Beale letters, from and about all her brothers and sisters to their mother at Tenterden, reflect that.

130. Beale Letters. Bundle X/1B/1.
131. She and her sister Fanny do not appear in the 1841 Census list for Homestall Farm.
132. Beale Letters. Bundle XI/C/1. Written at Homestall to grandmother Beale.
133. Beale Letters. Bundle XI/C/2.
134. Beale Letters. Bundle XI/C/3 and 4.
135. Beale Letters. Bundle XI/C/5 and 6.
136. Beale Letters. Bundle XII/D.
137. Governess of the small school two of the girls attended.
138. Beale Letters. Bundle XI/C/5-8.
139. Beale Letters. Bundle XI/D/5.
140. Census. TNA. This address was not listed after 1879/1881. E. A. Willats. Islington, Streets with a Story.
141. Census. TNA. On line. By 1886 this became 525-531 Holloway Road.
142. Will. Court 38. High Court, Strand, London.
143. Census. TNA. On line.
144. Beale Letters. Bundle XI/E/1.
145. Beale Letters. Bundle XI/E/1.
146. A daughter of Henry Hilton, who married Major William Augustus Munn of Throwley House, Throwley.
147. Beale Letters. Bundle XI/E/3.
148. Son in law and daughter of Henry Hilton who lived in Northumberland.
149. Beale Letters. Bundle XI/E/2.
150. Will. Court 38. High Court, Strand, London.
151. Beale Letters. Bundle XII/A14, A33 and A36.
152. Beale Letters. Bundle XI/A/1 and 2.
153. Beale Letters. Bundle XI/D/1.
154. Beale Letters. Bundle XI/A/1 and 2.
155. Beale Letters. Bundle XI/B/1.
156. Beale Letters. Bundle XI/B/4.
157. Beale Letters. Bundle VII/2.
158. Kelly's Directory. Authors library.
159. Sondes Rental. 1874. KHLC. Ref. U1175. E.118.
160. Beale Letters. Bundle XI/B/3.
161. Censuses 1891, 1901 and 1911. TNA. On line.
162. Will. Probate Office. London.
163. Beale Letters. Bundle XI/D/2.
164. Beale Letters. Bundle XI/D/3.
165. Beale Letters. Bundle XII/A/16.
166. Beale Letters. Bundle VIII/B/7.
167. One sixth of the £18,000 estate of Austen Neame, his wife's late father.
168. Census, TNA. On line. 1855 Post Office Directory. Kent. TNA.
169. J. Owen. The Shepherds of Shepherd Neame Brewery Faversham, 1732-1876. pp. 41-49 and 110.
170. Beale Letters. Bundle XI/E/1.
171. Census. 1841. TNA. On line.
172. Beale Letters. Bundle XI/C/5.
173. Beale Letters. Bundle XI/C/6.
174. Census. 1851. TNA. On line.
175. Post Office Directories. TNA.
176. Will 1886. Court 38, High Court, Strand.
177. Beale Letters. Bundle XI/D/3 and 5.
178. Beale Letters. Bundle XI/C/7.
179. Beale Letters. Bundle XI/B/1.
180. Census. TNA. On line.
181. Census. TNA. On line.
182. Post Office Directory. 1855. TNA.

Chapter Three

183. J. Owen. Op. Cit. For a fuller discussion of the period see Chapters 7 & 8.
184. As the Brewery Balance Books for 1859-1866 are missing this is based on the probate details of JH Mares. The amount corresponds with the known capital of £42,000 in 1867, which was calculated after further improvements had been made to the brewery. Balance Books 1867-1872. Shepherd Neame Brewery Archive.
185. Conveyance No 6. 30 July 1877. Mrs E M Shepherd to Percy Beale Neame. Shepherd Neame Archive.
186. See Chapter 2 above.
187. J. Owen. Op. Cit. Chapter 7 and Table 7.
188. Letter Book. December 1864-December 1871. Shepherd Neame Archive.
189. Letter Books of W. Maile. 1869-1872. 1872-1874. 1874-1879. Shepherd Neame Archive.
190. Journals. 1865-1872. 1872-1875. Shepherd Neame Archive.
191. J .Owen. Op. Cit. Chapter 8.
192. Faversham Post Office Directories 1859 and 1865. Authors collection.
193. The deeds have been lost by Swale Council.
194. J. Owen. Mount Ospringe. The House and it's Owners. 2001.
195. Census. 1851. TNA. On line.
196. Will. TNA. Ref. PROB11/2081. Death Duty Register. TNA. Ref. IR26/1815 f.649.
197. Will. TNA. Ref. PROB11/2252. Death Duty Register. TNA. Ref.
198. Will. See Chapter 1.
199. The 1866 Marriage Settlement has not survived in the Shepherd Neame Archive.
200. P. Selby. Op. Cit.
201. Notes and photographs taken by the author in 2005 when the house was gutted and divided into leasehold flats.
202. Cit. supra et Cit. ultra.
203. Census. TNA. On line. The Neames were staying at Oaklands, Border Road, Sydenham on the census day.
204. Wills. Court 38, High Court, The Strand, London.
205. Death Certificate. 22 December 1875. TNA.
206. Information with newspaper cuttings provided by his wife's great niece to the author.
207. J Owen. Op. Cit.

Chapter Four

208. Edward was the son of John Neame, the elder brother of Percy's father. Edward was also the brother of Harry Neame, the father of Percy's wife Florence.
209. Conveyances. July 1877. Shepherd Neame Archive.
210. This may explain why Percy insisted on bequeathing his widow such a generous life income from The Brewery in 1913.
211. Private Ledger. 1876-1899 . Shepherd Neame Archive.
212. J. Owen. Op. Cit. p.35.
213. J. Owen. Shepherds of Shepherd Neame. Op. Cit. pp.16-32 and Pedigree.

214. Balance Books. 1876-1913. Shepherd Neame Archive.

215. Private Ledger. Percy Beale Neame. 1876-1899. Freehold, Leasehold and Improvements sections. Repairs Ledger. 1876-1895. Shepherd Neame Archive.

216. Public Houses Trade. 1874-1908. Note Book. Shepherd Neame Archive.

217. Private Ledger. Plant and Utensils sections. Op. Cit.

218. Balance Books. Stores Ledgers sections. Op. Cit.

219. Keble's General Advertiser. 1890. Back page. Author's collection.

220. Stock Delivery Book. 1860-1899. Shepherd Neame Archive.

221. T R Gourvish & R G Wilson. The Brewing Industry. 1830-1980. pp.24-40.

222. See date stones on the buildings now the Tesco Store Faversham.

223. Victoria County History. Kent. Volume III.

224. Gourvish & Wilson. pp. 42-3. Op. Cit.

225. Stock Delivery Book. Op. Cit.

226. Stock Valuation Book. 1860-1913. Shepherd Neame Archive.

227. Letter Books. Out. 1875-1895. Shepherd Neame Archive.

228. J O'Donoghue, L Goulding and G Allen. Consumer Price Inflation since 1750. In Economic Trends 604. pp. 38-46.

229. See J Owen Shepherds of Shepherd Neame tables. Op. Cit.

230. Stock Delivery Book. Op. Cit.

231. See J Owen Shepherds of Shepherd Neame tables. pp.110-111. Op. Cit.

232. Balance Books. Op. Cit.

233. Private Ledger. Labour and Wages. Op. Cit.

234. Letter Books. 1876 onwards. Shepherd Neame Archive.

235. There are no employment lists for these dates. Information is taken from stray references in the Letter Books and Donations Lists in the hand of Percy Neame. 1877-1907. Ref. Box. E/1. Shepherd Neame Archive.

236. Bonus Sheets. Shepherd Neame Archive.

237. Donations Lists. Op. Cit.

238. Obituary. 22 August 1930. Faversham News. Microfilm. Faversham Library.

239. Faversham Census. 1881. Microfilm. National Archives and Faversham Library .

240. The Brewery Malt Books 1860-1866 and 1899 onwards survive. No Hop Books survive. Information on hops comes from The Stock Books 1876-1913 and The Journals 1876-1913. Shepherd Neame Archive.

241. Letter 13 December 1893. General Letter Book Out. 1893-1894. Shepherd Neame Archive.

242. Letter Book. 1894-1895. Shepherd Neame Archive.

243. Letter Book. 1885-1886.

244. Letter Book. 1892-1893.

245. Letter Book. 1893-1894.

246. Letter Book. 1891.

247. Letter Book. 1886-1887.

248. Letter Book. 1887-1888.

249. Letter Book. 1890-1891.

250. Letter Book. 1891-1892.

251. Letter Book. 1893-1894.

252. Letter Book. 1885-1886.

253. Letter Book. 1890-1891.

254. Letter Book. 1891-1892.

255. Letter Book. 1885.

256. Letter Book. 1885-1886.

257. Letter Book. 1888-1889.

258. Letter Book. 1893-1894.

259. Letter Book. 1889-1890.

260. Letter Book. 1888-1889.

261. Letter Book. 1885-1886.

262. Letter Book. 1885-1886.

263. Letter Book. 1887-1888.

264. Letter Book. 1887-1888. The Croft family lived locally at Doddinton Place, near Faversham.

265. Letter Book. 1888.

266. Letter Book. 1890-1891.

267. Letter Book. 1886.

268. Letter Book. 1888.

269. Letter Book. 1891-1892.

270. Letter Book. 1891-1892.

271. Adkins had suffered a stroke from which he never recovered. He moved from his house Newton Lodge, Newton Road to his son in Brighton in 1895. He died there in 1904.

272. Letter Books. 1887-1888.

273. Letter Book. 1886-1887.

274. Letter Book. 1887-1888.

275. Letter Book. 1894-1895.

276. Letter Book. 1890-1891.

277. Letter Book. 1885-1886.

278. Letter Book. 1892-1893.

279. Letter Book. 1887-1888.

280. Letter Book. 1888.

281. Subscription Book. 1884-1890. Country Brewers Association. Warwick University. Manuscript Collection. Ref. MSS 420.

282. Minute Book 3. 1868-1884. Op. Cit.

283. Letter Book. 1892.

284. Letter Book. 1892-1893.

285. Letter Book. 1892-1893.

286. Letter Book. 1885-1886.

287. Letter Book. 1886.

288. Letter Book. 1887.

289. Letter Book.1888.

290. Letter Book. 1892-1893.

291. Letter Book. 1886.

292. Letter Book. 1892-1893.

293. Obituary. 11 January 1911. Faversham Mercury. Faversham Library Microfilm.

Chapter Five

294. Balance Books. 1895-1912. Shepherd Neame Archive.

295. All in The Shepherd Neame Archive, Court Street, Faversham.

296. Balance Books. Op. Cit.

297. Balance Book. Op. Cit.

298. Private Ledger. 1899-1913.

299. Shepherd Neame Letter Book. 1910.

300. Private Ledger. 1899-1913.

301. Letter Book. 1891-1892.

302. Private Ledgers. 1876-1899. 1900-1913. Shepherd Neame Archive.

303. Private Ledgers. 1876-1913. Misc. Bills, Tenders and Correspondence. Box T.1. Shepherd Neame Archive. No specification of work carried out nor architects/contractors certificates survive.

304. I am grateful to Robin Duncan, Company Secretary, for pointing out the significance of numbering rooms at The Brewery. This was required by The Excise and discontinued only 30 years ago.

305. Private Ledger. 1899-1913.

306. All letters concerning these are from H S Neame. Letter Books. 1896 onwards.

307. Stock Delivery Book. 1860-1899. Shepherd Neame Archive. There are no barrelage figures between 1899 and 1920 in any Shepherd Neame records.

308. Gorvish and Wilson. p.24. Op. Cit.

309. Balance Book. 1912. Stock Book 1895.

310. Keble's General Advertiser. 1890. Authors Collection.

311. Stock Books. 1876-1913.

312. Letter Book. 1895.

313. Letter Book. 1896.

314. Letter Book. 1901.

315. Letter Book. 1901-1902.

316. 1903 List. Shepherd Neame Archive. 5 January 1907. Advertisement. Faversham News.

317. The Brewery Archive has a very large collection of these which often contain business plans correspondence and building specifications.

318. Loans Book. 1910-1930. Shepherd Neame Archive.

319. Clubs Trade Book. 1906-1960. Shepherd Neame Archive. This is the earliest ledger about clubs.

320. Letters In. Travellers Files. 1900-. Shepherd Neame Archive.

321. Clubs Trade Book. Op. Cit.

322. The Croft family built and lived at Doddington Place, near Faversham.

323. Letter Book. 1887-1888.

324. Letter from George Borman. Letter Book. 1892.

325. Letter from William Maile. 20 February 1892. Letter Book

326. Letter Book. 1895-1896.

327. Letter Book. 1899-1900.

328. Letter Book. 1904. Letter 4 May 1904.

329. Letter Book. 1908-1909. Letter 18 March 1909.

330. Letter Book. 1912. Letter dated 7 May 1912.

331. Public Houses Trade Book. 1876-1908. Shepherd Neame Archive.

332. 1 barrel contained 288 pints of beer.

333. No ledgers of the Bottled Beer Department survive in the Shepherd Neame Archive for this time.

334. Advertising List. 1897. Shepherd Neame Archive.

335. Price Lists. 1910. Shepherd Neame Archive.

336. Letter Books. 1892-1913. A collection of copper measures used has survived at The Brewery.

337. Letter Book. 1897.

338. Letter Book. 1900.

339. Letter Book 1903.

340. Plans and Accounts. Shepherd Neame Archive. 1905.

341. This building survives but has been converted into flats.

342. Balance Books. Op. Cit.

343. Letter Book. 1904-1905.

344. Letter. Employment Files. E2/10. Shepherd Neame Archive.

345. Faversham News. 29 June 1907. Faversham Library.

346. Letter Book. 1901-1902.

347. Obituary. Op. Cit.

348. Miscellaneous Boxes. Shepherd Neame Archive.

349. Miscellaneous Boxes. Shepherd Neame Archive.

350. Always known as Useless Neame in the family.

351. Letter Book. 1910.

352. Agreement. 1893. Percy B Neame Trunk 1. Shepherd Neame Archive.

353. Dozens of letters about the farms survive in the General Out Letter Books.

354. Obituary. Op. Cit.

355. I am grateful to David Robertson Hon. Archivist of KCCC at Canterbury for extracting this information.

356. Letter Book. 1908-1909.

357. J H A Barnes recollections in The Barnes Saga. pp. 193-196. I am grateful to George Barnes for showing me this family book.

358. Neame Pedigree. Prideaux Selby. Faversham Farmers Club. p.114. Neame Pedigree attached.

359. Demolished, except for the garage and squash court, in 1973 and replaced by houses. SE corner of The Mall.

360. Mrs Mary Dawes. Conversations with the author.

361. J A Venn. Cambridge Alumni.

362. Obituary. Faversham News. 8 July 1916. Faversham Library. Microfilm.

363. 1911. Census. TNA.

364. Harry Neame Deed Boxes . Letters files. Shepherd Neame Archive.

365. There are no service records for him at TNA.

366. 2 October 1956. Company Secretary Letter Book 9. 1953-1962. Shepherd Neame Archive.

367. Will. Probate Office. Court 38. The Strand.

368. The Barns Saga. Op. Cit. Much of the personal information is taken from JAH Barnes memoirs.

369. The National Archives. Kew. Ref. WR/261919. Dover Marine Station. Roll of Honour. 1914-1918.

Chapter Six

370. Obituary. Op. Cit.

371. This settlement is summarised in the submission of Reginald Mason the London Accountant of The Brewery to the Chancery Division of the High Court 'In the matter of the estate of Percy Beale Neame deceased. Between C L Graham, Plaintiff and H S Neame, Defendant. 1914 N No 707.' This with a large collection of supporting papers and correspondence survives in Trunk 1. Shepherd Neame Archive.

372. Trunk 1. Shepherd Neame Archive.

373. Board Minute Books. 1914-date. Shepherd Neame Archive.

374. His practice, at 55 East Street, was taken over in 1916 by Dr Porter, who in turn was succeeded by Dr Roy Edney in 1948. It continues today at The Health Centre, Bank Street in the name of Dr Moore.

375. The Barnes Saga. Op. Cit. Mary Dawes said that he never came to Kent after marriage.

376. Military record. Ref: ADM/196/62. TNA. Kew.

377. Obituaries. Hampshire Telegraph, Post and Naval Chronicle. Evening News. 1 May 1940. Gosport Library.

Illustrations

Fig. 1   *Percy Beale Neame*
c. 1880

Fig. 2   *Harry Sidney Neame*
c. 1915

Fig. 3   *Alick Percy Neame*
          c. 1910

Fig. 4   *Arthur Neame*
          c. 1910

Fig. 5   *Charles Lawrence Graham*
c. 1920

Fig. 6   *William Maile*
c. 1869

Fig. 7   *George Ernest Boorman*
             c. 1915

Fig. 8   *William Eustace Neame*
             c. 1940

Fig. 13   *The Brewhouse*
          c. 1900

Fig. 14   *Malt Grinder*
          c. 1900

Fig. 15 *Mash Tuns 1A & 1B*
            c. 1900

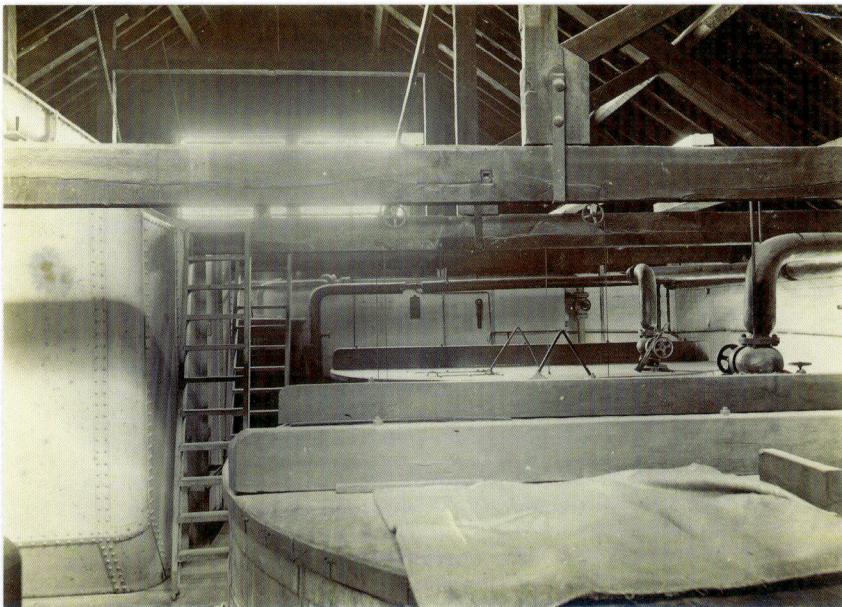

Fig. 16 *Grist Case and Hot Liquor Tanks*
            c. 1900

Fig. 17   *Copper No 2 for Wort*
                c. 1900

Fig. 18   *Beer Storage Tanks Nos 1-4*
                c.1900

Fig. 19   *Filters*
            c. 1910

Fig. 20   *Bottling Hall*
            c. 1910

Fig. 21   *Cask Store and Cleaning Shed*
            c. 1900

Fig. 22   *Cask Store and Cleaning Shed*
            c. 1900

Fig. 23   *Plans of Wine and Spirit Store*
               1905

Fig. 24   *Front Office Interior*
               17 Court Street
               c. 1915

Fig. 25   *Office Exterior*
          17 Court Street
          1895

COURT STREET, FAVERSHAM.

5731 The "Wyndham" Series.

Fig. 26   *Office Exterior*
16 & 17 Court Street
c. 1900

Fig. 27 *John Neame*
c. 1820

Fig. 28 *George Neame*
c. 1870

Fig. 29 *Anne Neame (nee Beale later Hilton)*
c. 1845

Fig. 30 *Henry Hilton*
c. 1845

Fig. 31   *Austen Beale Neame*
          c. 1850

Fig. 32   *Percy Beale Neame*
          c. 1850

Fig. 33   *Percy Beale Neame 'The Master'*
           c. 1895

Fig. 34   *Florence Neame 'Madame'*
           c. 1900

Fig. 35   *Major Charles Oliver Graham*
c. 1935

Fig. 36   *Pte. Percy Alric Churchward*
1915

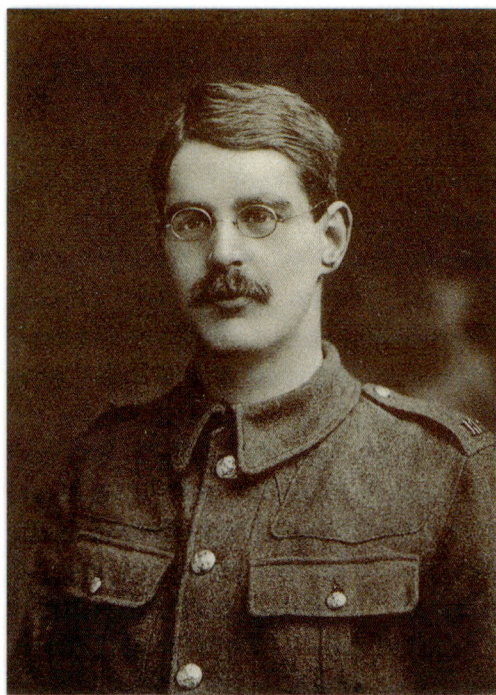

Fig. 37 *Unidentified Neame Daughters*
c. 1890

Fig. 38   Madame
The Mount
c. 1900

Fig. 39   *Unidentified Neame Family*
                The Mount
                c. 1910

Fig. 40   *Unidentified Neame Family*
                The Mount
                c. 1900

Fig. 41   *Madame at London Zoo*
           With grandchildren
           c. 1925

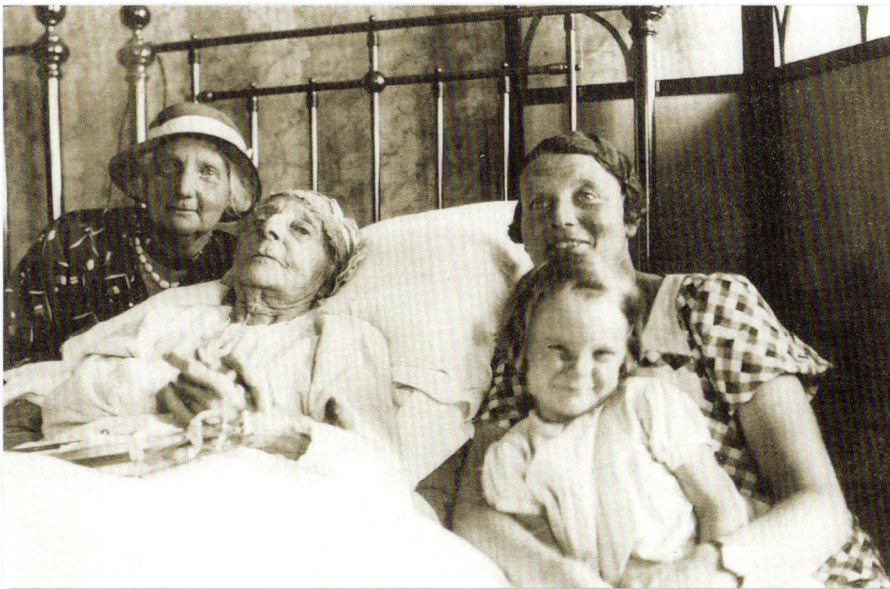

Fig. 42   *Madame near the End*
           With Ida Cotterill and Family
           c. 1932

Fig. 43 *Drill Hall (Assembly Rooms) Faversham*
Arthur Neame in Foreground
c. 1910

Fig. 44   *Harry Sidney Neame Wedding*
            Margate
            1899

Fig. 45   *Arthur Neame Funeral*
               Ospringe Church
               1916

Fig. 46   *Arthur Neame*
               Officer's Commendation Medal
               1916

Fig. 47 *Cricket Match*
The Mount
Percy Neame centre; William Maile bottom right
c. 1875

Fig. 48   *Cricket Match*
The Mount
Arthur Neame centre
1906

Fig. 49   *Canterbury Cricket Week*
             1906

"The Mount", Faversham. May 5th, 1882.

Fig. 56 *The Mount, Faversham*
Percy Neame and Family
1882

Fig. 57   *Sole Street, Selling*

Fig. 58   *The Mount, Faversham*
Winter
c. 1900

Fig. 59   *Memorial Window*
           Goodnestone-next-Faversham Church
           Austen Neame
           c. 1837

Fig. 60   *Graves*
Percy Beale Neame, Bernard Neame and Mary Anne Neame
Ospringe Church
Whiting of Faversham
1877, 1900 and 1913

Plan

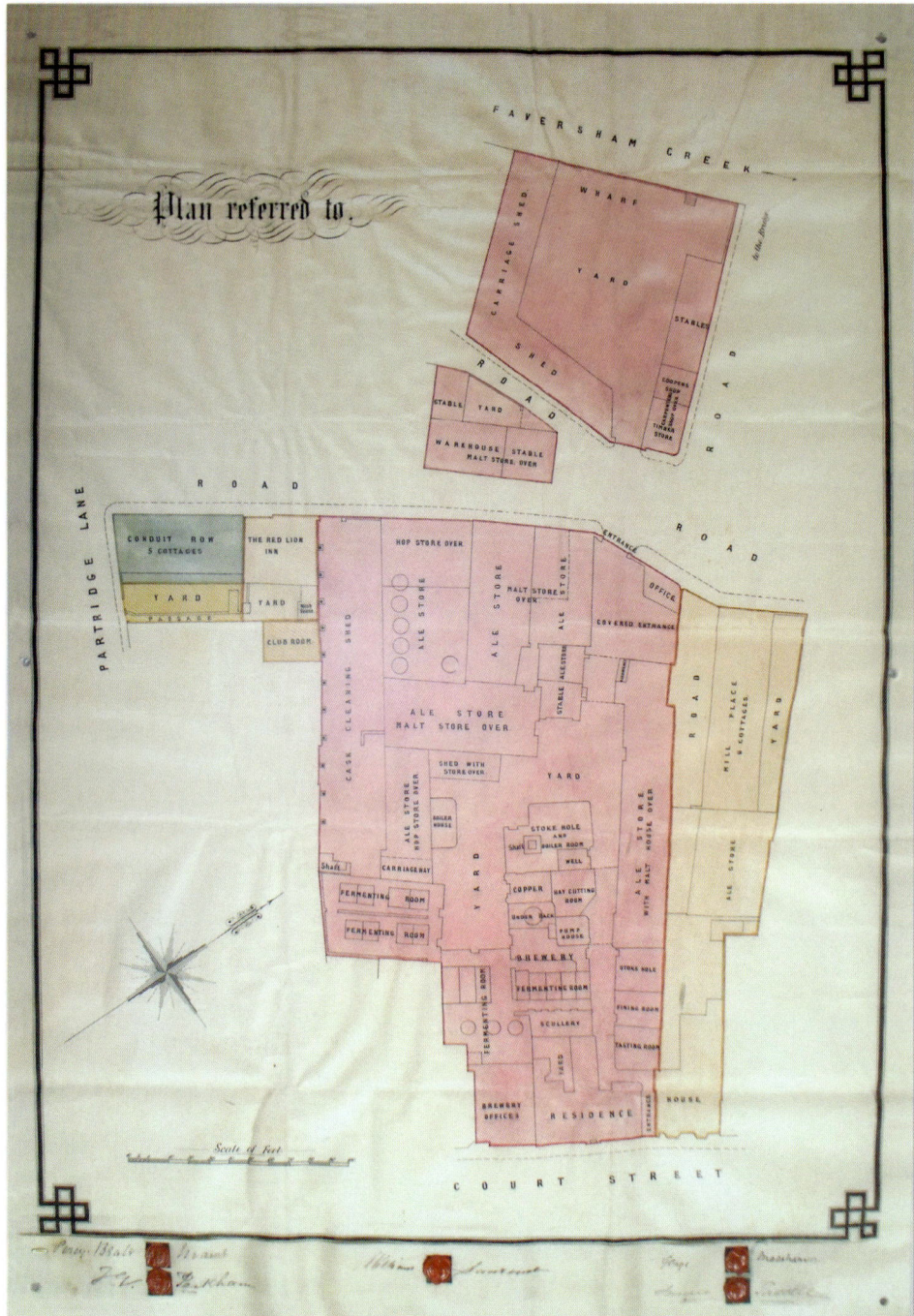

Plan. 1 *The Brewery Site*
1897

Tables

Table 1. *Local and National Population and Brewing Statistics 1871 - 1913*

Dates	Population of Faversham, Preston & Ospringe	Production of Shepherd Neame Barrels p.a.	Production UK Barrels p.a.	Consumption Per capita UK Gallons p.a.
1871	11078			
1875-1879			28.2m	40.5
1877/1878		43142		
1878/1879		39056		
1880/1881		34055		
1880-1884			25.0m	33.6
1881	13041			
1882/1883		32258		
1884/1885		34752		
1885-1889			25.5m	32.5
1886/1887		33154		
1888/1889		33004		
1890/1891		31720		
1890-1894			27.7m	33.4
1891	14157			
1892/1893		34366		
1894/1895		35543		
1895-1899			30.3m	34.5
1896/1897		36562		
1898/1899		40497		
1899/1900		39612		
1900-1904			30.6m	34.3
1901	14883			
1905-1909			28.7m	30.9
1910-1914			28.9m	29.4
1911	13920			

Source: *Victoria County History. Kent.*
Shepherd Neame Stock Delivery Book 1860-1899.
British Brewing Industry. Gourvish & Wilson.

Table 2. *Shepherd Neame Abbreviated Balance and Profit & Loss Books 1875-1912*

	S&N	PBN								
Years	**1875**	**1878**	**1880**	**1885**	**1890**	**1895**	**1900**	**1905**	**1910**	**1912**
CREDITS										
Freehold/Leasehold Estate	86763	94489	101147	108361	124691	135962	176600	200742	203707	200398
Stock/Plant/Rent/Cash/Loans/Etc.	59311	64691	69573	73232	69376	68091	76695	82162	80470	89287
Bad Debts		-1916	-2294	-3136	-2272	-1661	-904	-1716	-4365	-6509
Goodwill	10000	10000	10000	10000	10000	10000	10000	10000	10000	10000
Total	156074	167264	178426	188457	201795	212392	262391	291188	289812	293176
DEBITS										
Mortgages/Loans	50408	77469	78495	63074	56059	59359	83113	102543	98103	104575
Trade/Other	3460	1758	1517	2851	2684	1307	2077	3096	2861	5568
Interest on Capital to Partner(s)	4584	3578	4392	5600	6591	6779	7872	8377	8891	8649
Net Profit to Partner(s)	5932	12889	6185	4937	4632	8337	10709	8204	784	1406
Capital Balance (Net Assets)	91690	71570	87837	111995	131829	135572	157447	167551	177828	172978
Inland Revenue		0	0	0	0	1038	1173	1417	1345	0
Total	156074	167264	178426	188457	201795	212392	262391	291188	289812	293176

PROFIT AND LOSS ACCOUNTS

CREDITS (Turnover)										
Sales/Beer/Malt/Barley/Wine/Spirits	82108	82933	69903	65639	62862	65295	88953	97362	89025	99701
Rents	1744	2038	2414	2645	2628	2467	3448	3683	3589	3407
Stock/Malt/Hops/Beer	17676	18254	22925	33175	18694	11990	13741	15045	18416	18535
MALT/BEER DUTY & LICENCES		9237	9509	10172	10129	10728	13031	14350	13339	14484
NET PROFIT										
Interest on Capital Paid to Partner(s)	4584	3578	4392	5600	6591	6779	7872	8377	8891	8649
Interest Paid to HS, A & A Neame									1869	1946
Net Profit Paid to Partner(s)	5932	12889	6185	4937	4632	8337	10709	8204	783	1406
Interest Paid as % Net Assets	5%	5%	5%	5%	5%	5%	5%	5%	5%	5%
Profit Paid as % of Net Assets	6.40%	17.40%	7%	4.40%	3.50%	6.20%	6.80%	4.90%	0.40%	0.80%

Source: *Balance Books 1875-1913*
Shepherd Neame Archive

Table 3. *Shepherd Neame Nubers of Public Houses 1848-1913*

Dates	Faversham, Preston & Ospringe		Villages		London Road		Towns		Sheppey		TOTALS		TOTAL NUMBER
	FH	LH	FH	LH	FH	LH	FH	LH	FH	LH	FH	LH	
1848	11	1	14	1	8	0	5	0	0	0	38	2	40
1865	20	4	17	21	9	14	9	12	0	23	55	74	129
1876	19	4	23	9	10	11	7	4	0	11	59	39	98
1885	19	4	24	8	10	6	14	2	2	5	69	25	94
1895	20	4	29	12	14	4	16	1	3	3	82	24	106
1905	21	4	31	12	16	3	17	0	6	2	91	21	112
1913	19	4	32	12	16	4	17	0	6	2	90	22	112

FH: Freehold Houses
LH: Leasehold houses

Source: *Deeds Ledger*
          Rent Ledgers
          Shepherd Neame Archives

Table 4. *Shepherd Neame Public Houses 1876-1913*

Faversham, Preston, Ospringe & Davington

Date Acquired	Date Disposed	Pub	LH
1711		Castle	
1715		Three Tuns	
1736		Bear	
1769		Anchor	LH
1771		Queens Head	
1778		Red Lion	
1784		Smack/Kings Head	
1789		White Horse	
1796		Anchor (Ospringe)	
1844		Sun	
1845		Lion (Ospringe)	
1846		Crown & Anchor	
1850		Mechanics Arms	
1853	1912	Shakespeare	
1856	1912	Royal Standard	
1858		Railway	LH
1860		Elephant & Castle	LH
1860		St Annes Cross	
1860		Windmill (Preston)	
1861	1912	Masons Arms	
1863		Market Inn	
1863		Royal William	
1865		Shipwrights Arms	LH
1892		Cherry Tree (Preston)	
1900		Willow Tap (Brents)	
1908		Alma (Ospringe)	

Villages

Date Acq.	Date Disp.	Pub	Place	LH
1749		Three Horse Shoes	Hernhill	
1750		Carpenters Arms	Eastling	
1755		Plough	Lewson Street	
1775		Artichoke	Chartham	
1778		Chequer	Lenham	
1778		Kings Arms	South Street	
1786		George	Newnham	
1786		Three Mariners	Oare	
1801		Plough	Stalisfield	
1821		Bull	Lenham Heath	
1834	1892	Wheel	Westwell	LH
1840		Star	Chilham	
1843		Fox & Hounds	Chislet	
1852		Royal Oak	Mersham	
1860		Sportsmans Arms	Egerton	
1860	1893	Flying Horse	Wye	LH?
1860		Bull	Bethersden	LH
1860	1902	Woolpack	Smeeth	LH?
1860		Woolpack	Chilham	LH?
1861		Sondes Arms	Selling	LH
1862	1883	Golden Ball	Kennington	LH
1864		Fox	Oversland	LH
1865		Chequers	Doddington	LH
1865		Hampton Oyster	Hampton	
1865		Windmill	Luddenham	LH
1866		Crown & Anchor	Willsborough	
1870		Beer House	Sheldwich	
1872		Walnut Tree	Aldington	
1872		Bonny Cravat	Woodchurch	
1873		Red Lion	Charing Heath	
1874		Beacon Court	Gillingham	
1884		Dove	Dargate	
1886		Rose & Forge	Kennington	
1885		Olive Branch	Borden	
1886		Griffins Head	Chillenden	LH
1887		Prince of Wales	Hoath	
1888		Unicorn	Beakesbourne	LH
1889		Gate	Marshside Chislet	
1893		Lord Nelson	Waltham	LH
1893		Palm Tree	Elham	LH
1894		New Inn	Murston	
1894		Acorn	Birchington	LH
1895		George	Leeds	LH
1896		Evenhill House	Littlebourne	
1897		Crown	Sarre	
1898		Park Gate	Leeds	LH
1898		White Lion	Selling	LH
1908		Old Century	Selling	

London Road

Date Acq.	Date	Pub Disp.	Place	LH
1750		Dolphin	Boughton	
1750		Bell	Sittingbourne	
1750		Dover Castle	Greenstreet	
1770		White Hart	Newington	
1798		Queens Head	Boughton	
1808		Shakespeare	Canterbury	
1844		Prince Albert	Canterbury	
1846		White Horse	Boughton	
1855		Rose	Sittingbourne	LH
1857		Fountain	Sittingbourne	LH
1857		Globe & Engine	Sittingbourne	LH
1860		Park Tavern	Sittingbourne	
1860		Prince of Wales	Sittingbourne	LH?
1860		Whitehall	Harbledown	LH
1860		Three Post Boys	Sittingbourne	LH?
1863		Don Jon	Canterbury	LH
1864		Leigh Arms	Newington	LH FH1894
1875		Monarch	Gillingham	
1876		Plough & Harrow	Bridge	
1889		Greyhound	Rochester	
1892		Mackland Arms	Rainham	
1900		Coach & Horses	Canterbury	
1906		Chandos	Dover	
1906		Green Dragon	Dover	LH

123

Table 4. *Shepherd Neame Public Houses 1876-1913 (cont.)*

Towns

Date Acq.	Date Disp.	Pub	Place	LH
1787		Castle	Ashford	
1836		Falstaff	Ramsgate	
1847		Beaver	Ashford	
1850		West Cliffe Brewery	Ramsgate	
1860		Victoria	Ashford	LH FH1898
1860		Milton Arms	Milton	
1860	1904	Jolly Sailor	Milton	LH
1863		Richmond Tavern	Herne Bay	
1866		Railway Hotel	Herne Bay	
1873		Smack	Whitstable	LH FH1880
1876		Prince Alfred	Milton Regis	
1878		Duke of Cumberland	Whitstable	
1879		Four Horseshoes	Whitstable	
1879		Prince of Wales	Herne Bay	
1882		Coach & Horses	Whitstable	
1883		East Kent Hotel	Whitstable	
1883		Rising Sun	Whitstable	
1887		Rose	Herne Bay	

Isle of Sheppy

Date Acq.	Date Disp.	Pub	Place	LH
1856		Druids Arms	Sheerness	LH FH1900
1858		British Queen	Minster	LH FH1869
1858		Fountain Hotel	Sheerness	LH FH1865
1861	1895	Globe	Elmley	LH
1861		Napier Tavern	Sheerness	LH FH1890
1863		Blacksmiths Arms	Sheerness	LH
1874		Steam Reserve	Sheerness	LH
1897		Watermans Arms	Sheerness	
1898		Hero of Crimea	Sheerness	

Source: *Deeds Register.*
1864 Mortgages to Mares Executors.
1875 Mortgages to Shepherd Executors.
Rent Book 1865/75
Sun Insurance Co

Table 5. *Shepherd Neame Productuion Lines 1848-1813*

	1848	1858	1868	1875	1880	1885	1890	1895	1900	1905	1910	1913
Pale Ale			*	*	*	*	*	*	*	*	*	*
Pale Ale No 1			*									
Pale Ale No 2			*									
Bitter Beer		*	*	*	*	*	*	*	*	*	*	*
AK						*	*	*	*	*	*	*
Mild Beer			*	*	*	*	*	*	*	*	*	*
Porter	*	*	*	*	*	*	*	*	*	*	*	*
Stout			*	*	*	*	*	*	*	*	*	*
Stout Porter	*											
Table Beer	*	*	*	*	*	*	*	*				
Table Ale									*	*	*	*
X		*						*	*	*	*	*
XX	*		*									
XXX Ale	*											
Stock Ale		*	*		*	*	*	*	*	*	*	*
London Porter			*			*	*	*	*	*	*	*
London D Stout			*			*	*	*	*	*	*	*
S Stout			*									
D Stout			*									
Mild Ale		*										
Meux D Stout		*										
Meux S Stout		*										
Porter		*										
Ale				*	*	*	*	*		*	*	*
LDA											*	*
Total	5	8	15	7	8	11	11	12	12	13	14	14

Source: *Balance Books 1848-1913*

Pedigrees

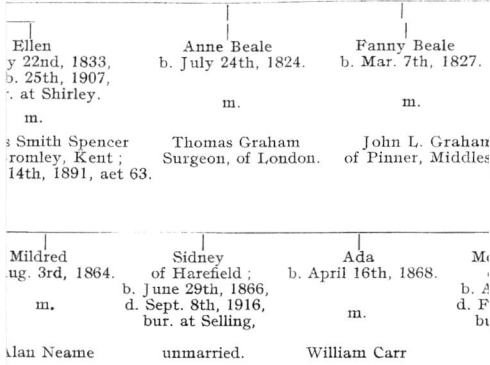

Ellen
y 22nd, 1833,
b. 25th, 1907,
r. at Shirley.

m.

s Smith Spencer
romley, Kent ;
14th, 1891, aet 63.

Anne Beale
b. July 24th, 1824.

m.

Thomas Graham
Surgeon, of London.

Fanny Beale
b. Mar. 7th, 1827.

m.

John L. Graham
of Pinner, Middles

Mildred
ug. 3rd, 1864.

m.

Alan Neame

Sidney
of Harefield ;
b. June 29th, 1866,
d. Sept. 8th, 1916,
bur. at Selling,

unmarried.

Ada
b. April 16th, 1868.

m.

William Carr

M
b. A
d. F
bu

PEDIGREE o

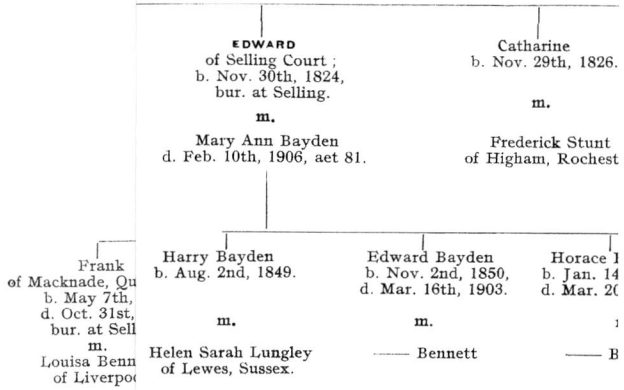

EDWARD
of Selling Court ;
b. Nov. 30th, 1824,
bur. at Selling.

m.

Mary Ann Bayden
d. Feb. 10th, 1906, aet 81.

Catharine
b. Nov. 29th, 1826.

m.

Frederick Stunt
of Higham, Rochest

Frank
of Macknade, Qu
b. May 7th,
d. Oct. 31st,
bur. at Sell
m.
Louisa Benn
of Liverpo

Harry Bayden
b. Aug. 2nd, 1849.

m.

Helen Sarah Lungley
of Lewes, Sussex.

Edward Bayden
b. Nov. 2nd, 1850,
d. Mar. 16th, 1903.

m.

——— Bennett

Horace I
b. Jan. 14
d. Mar. 2(

——— B

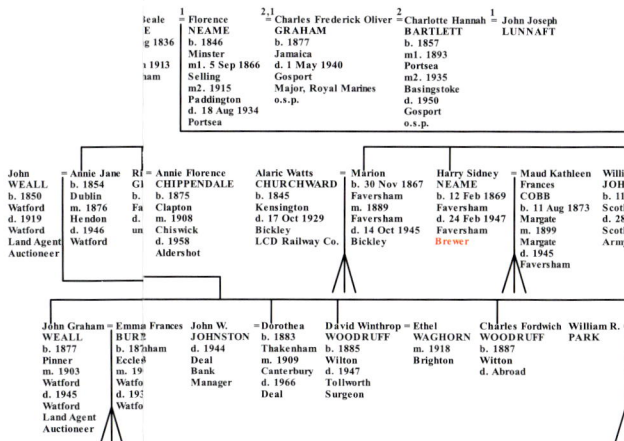

	1	2,1	2	1
Beale	= Florence NEAME	= Charles Frederick Oliver GRAHAM	= Charlotte Hannah BARTLETT	= John Joseph LUNNAFT
E	b. 1846	b. 1877	b. 1857	
g 1836	Minster	Jamaica	m1. 1893	
	m1. 5 Sep 1866	d. 1 May 1940	Portsea	
1913	Selling	Gosport	m2. 1935	
ham	m2. 1915	Major, Royal Marines	Basingstoke	
	Paddington	o.s.p.	d. 1950	
	d. 18 Aug 1934		Gosport	
	Portsea		o.s.p.	

John WEALL	= Annie Jane	R	= Annie Florence CHIPPENDALE	Alaric Watts CHURCHWARD	= Marion	Harry Sidney NEAME	= Maud Kathleen Frances COBB	Willi JOH
b. 1850	b. 1854	G	b. 1875	b. 1845	b. 30 Nov 1867	b. 12 Feb 1869	b. 11 Aug 1873	b. 11
Watford	Dublin	b.	Clapton	Kensington	Faversham	Faversham	Margate	Scotl
d. 1919	m. 1876	Fa	m. 1908	d. 17 Oct 1929	m. 1889	d. 24 Feb 1947	m. 1899	d. 28
Watford	Hendon	d.	Chiswick	Bickley	Faversham	Faversham	Margate	Scotl
Land Agent	d. 1946	un	d. 1958	LCD Railway Co.	d. 14 Oct 1945	Brewer	d. 1945	Army
Auctioneer	Watford		Aldershot		Bickley		Faversham	

John Graham WEALL	= Emma Frances BUR?	John W. JOHNSTON	= Dorothea	David Winthrop WOODRUFF	= Ethel WAGHORN	Charles Fordwich WOODRUFF	William R. PARK
b. 1877	b. 18?ham	d. 1944	b. 1883	b. 1885	m. 1918	b. 1887	
Pinner	Eccle?	Deal	Thakenham	Wilton	Brighton	Witton	
m. 1903	m. 19	Bank	m. 1909	d. 1947		d. Abroad	
Watford	Watfo	Manager	Canterbury	Tollworth			
d. 1945	d. 19?		d. 1966	Surgeon			
Watford	Watfo		Deal				
Land Agent							
Auctioneer							

:hard Beale, of Bid-
ιden, gent. bo. 9th
t. 1668, ob. 10th
Nov. 1757.

| =Edward Curteis, of Tenterden, Esq. | Elizabeth Beale, bo. 6th October, 1709, mar. 1st Dec. 1731. | =J. Haffend of Tenterd gent. |

Descendents living in Gloucester:

| Charles Beale, bo. 1804. | Frances Beale, bo. 1807. | Elizabeth Be bo. 1809 |

Index